GROWING NEW CHURCHES

STEP-BY-STEP PROCEDURES IN NEW CHURCH PLANTING

CARL W. MOORHOUS
Foreword by Paul Benjamin

Carl W. Moorhous, Evangelist

First Printing, 1975
Second Printing, 1976
Third Printing, 1983

GROWING NEW CHURCHES

© Carl Moorhous 1975
Printed in the U.S.A.
All rights reserved.

Library of Congress Catalog Card No. 75—13333

DEDICATED
With Love
To My Wife
Thelma

CONTENTS

Newcomers
Advertising
Religious Survey
Door-to-Door Visitation
Institutional Visitation
Daily Vacation Bible School
Families in Need
Weddings, Funerals, etc.
Bible Study Groups
Permanent and Supportive Members
Analyzing

Co-ordinator (Superintendent)
Records
Opening Services
Classroom Space

Musically
Bulletins
Communion Ware, Offering Plates, etc.
Worship
Furniture
Records
Nursery
Office Equipment

Benefits
Preparation
Church-Related Organs
Newspapers
Throw-aways
Brochures
Radio
Television
Introductory Posters

Satisfaction
Tithes and Offerings
Tithing for Missions
Stewardship Program
Support for Minister-Evangelist
Mother Church
Self-supporting
Evangelistic Fellowship

Importance of Proper Site
Size
Parking
Title Matters
Testings
Orientation of Buildings
Architect
Church Builders
Contractors

Building Committee
Construction Warnings
  Over Building
  Under Building
  Building Permits
  Changes
  Insurance
  Neglect of Evangelism
  Waiver of Lien

FOREWORD

Carl Moorhous and I have been friends for a quarter of a century. During this period of time, I have watched him develop into one of the foremost church planters in America.

His record to date is nearly fifty new congregations in which he has either assisted or carried the primary role.

Carl has the heart of an evangelist. He lives and breathes church growth. His vocation and his avocation is planting new churches so that more of God's lost children may be found.

This book serves a very practical function. It can be an extremely useful tool to all those who are interested in church growth through new church planting. Every chapter is designed to give guidelines on a phase of development in the life of a new church.

I heartily recommend this study to all those who labor in the fields that are white unto harvest.

Paul Benjamin, director
National Church Growth Research Center
Box 3760
Washington, D. C. 20007

PREFACE

This book, Step-by-Step Procedures in New Church Planting, has not been written by a professional writer, in the true sense of the word professional. It is my first book (hopefully, not my last) written by me, Carl Moorhous, a mere mortal who has dedicated his life to Christ and His work here on earth. Never before in time has there been such a need for Christ and the Church, and to bring people back to the love, fellowship, understanding and peace that can be found only in Christ. Thus, in writing this book, it is with the hope of reaching others, to help them in the planting of new churches and the continuance of God's work.

In summary, let me quote from Chapter VI, of this book, "What Makes a Great Church? It's . . . not big budgets, but big hearts; not money received, but the services rendered; not tall buildings, but lofty visions; not record-breaking attendance, but God's presence; not frantic motions, but dedicated action; not soft seats and bright lights, but courageous leadership and true followers; not loud talking, but quiet doing; not members in beautiful clothes, but members living godly lives; not preachers telling it their way, but teachers stressing the truth and living thereby; not actions in the past, but things being done **NOW**."

ACKNOWLEDGEMENTS

Across the years there have been many influences on my life that have led to the writing of this book.

Besides accepting Christ as my Saviour and the influence of a Christian mother and a loving father (who accepted Christ in later years), I am first of all indebted to Lincoln Christian College and Chancellor Earl C. Hargrove and the faculty members who taught me wisely and patiently.

I am very grateful also for my living-link church, the First Christian Church of Clinton, Ill. and my brother in Christ, Mr. Winston Zastrow, the senior minister. Together they have inspired me and assisted me in many areas. Mr. Zastrow has counseled and encouraged me through the months I have struggled with this book.

Appreciation must be expressed to my many associates in the Chicago District Evangelistic Association. Many of the ideas and suggestions in this book have been tried and proven through them. Such men as Robert Sloniger, Calvin Phillips, Richard Hazeltine, Harry Brooker, George Nelson, Donald Parrish and a large host of others are a never ending source of friendship and strength in my labors in the Lord as His Churches are planted.

My wife, Thelma, and I began working with new churches early in our marriage and she has always been as enthusiastic and dedicated to the task as I.

To Paul Benjamin and Knofel Staton I am very grateful. They have urged and encouraged me in preparing and writing this study.

Appreciation must be expressed to my sister-in-law, Mrs. Rosalie Gilliland, who painstakenly edited and proofread my manuscript, and to S. Edward Tesh, professor at Lincoln Christian Seminary, Lincoln, Illinois, who proofed the final copy of the book.

I

CHURCH PLANTING IN THE NEW TESTAMENT

 A careful examination of the New Testament will clearly establish the church as Christ's "vehicle" for saving, consolidating, and preserving God's people. Jesus Christ, God's only begotten Son, spoke about the viable and enduring nature of His church when He said, "I will build My church; and the gates of Hades shall not overpower it" (Matthew 16:18). Jesus was, of course speaking of a people and not another building that would equal or rival the temple of Jerusalem.

Several years later, in Jerusalem, after Christ had ascended to heaven and the Holy Spirit had descended upon the apostles, Peter was preaching. He was under the guidance of the Holy Spirit (Acts 2:1-33). As sinful men were being accused of rejecting God and crucifying His Son, the Messiah, they cried out with guilt stricken consciences, "Brethren, what shall we do?" (Acts 2:37). Peter then told them, "Repent, and let each of you be baptized in the name of Jesus Christ for the forgiveness of your sins: and you shall receive the gift of the Holy Spirit" (Acts 2:38). Three thousand souls were **added** that day (Acts 2:41), "And the Lord was **adding** to their number day by day those who were being saved" (Acts 2:47). The church, the people of God, was being extended and multiplied.

It seems obvious in this study of the New Testament that Christ was establishing His church. The idea of establishing a "Spiritual Beachhead" in the world is very descriptive when we realize the church is at war, not against flesh and blood, but against "spiritual forces of wickedness in the heavenly places" (Ephesians 6:12). The church was established to combat Satan's influence and to release his hold on all the peoples of the world. (Matthew 28:18-20; Mark 16:15-16; Luke 24:46-53; Acts 1:4-14). The church, therefore, must be planted today in all areas and all communities.

1

The planting of churches in the New Testament is most clearly outlined in the book of Acts.

1. The Jewish growth pattern....Jerusalem of Judea...Acts 2:1-8:4.

2. The Jewish-Gentile extension....Samaritans...Acts 8:5-25.

3. Special ministry of Philip....preaching to the Ethiopian Eunuch and to the cities....Acts 8:26-40.

4. The Gentile church planted through special revelation....Joppa—Caesarea....Acts 10:1-11:18.

5. Planting new churches....Acts 13:1-28:31.
   a. Churches planted in Asia Minor Cities: Salamis, Acts 13:5; Paphos, 13:9-11; Perga, 13:13; Antioch of Syria, 13:16-41; Iconium, 13:50-51; Lystra, 14:5-6, 8-19; Derbe, 14:20; Attalia, 14:25; Troas, 16:9 (2nd trip); Ephesus, 18:18-19.
   b. Churches established on the European Continent: Philippi, Acts 16:11-12; Thessalonica, 16:40-17:1; Berea, 17:10-11; Athens, 17:14-15; Corinth, 18:1-17.
   c. Paul to Rome and his letters to the now established churches: Acts 23:31-28:31.

Other New Testament Scriptures help to explain the strategic need for the church. It is for this reason that Christ died for His church (Ephesians 5:25). "There is therefore now no **condemnation** for those who are **in** Christ Jesus" (Romans 8:1).

1. "For even as the **body** is one and yet has many members, and all the members of the **body,** though they are many, are one **body,** so also is Christ. For by one Spirit we were all **baptized** into one **body,** whether Jews or Greeks, whether slaves or free, . . ." (I Corinthians 12:12-13). (Bold type is mine.)

2. "Therefore you are no longer a **slave,** but a **son;** and if a **son,** then an **heir** through God" (Galatians 4:7).

3. "And He put all things in subjection under His feet, and gave Him as head over all things to the church, which is His **body,** the fulness of Him who fills all in all. But God, being rich in mercy, because of His great love with which He loved us (John 3:16) even when we were **dead** in our **transgressions,** made us **alive** together with Christ, . . . (Ephesians 1:22-23, 2:4-5).

Christ's redeeming mission on earth (Matthew 1:21; Luke 19:10; I Timothy 1:15) was to be accomplished through the church, His body, as men had faith in Him and turned from their sins to Him and were baptized into Christ (Acts 2:37-38, 47; Romans 6:3-5).

Our sinful world must have Christ's Church! It is God's answer or solution to the all-consuming power of Satan. Recognition by God's people must be given to the power of the gospel (Romans 1:15-17) as it is extended into all communities.

2

There will be many blessings and advantages in establishing another church as a "Spiritual Beachhead" for Christ. (1) New strength in **leadership** will be developed in the new church as well as in the "Mother" church, if one is involved. (2) A new church will make it possible to conduct total-indepth **evangelization** of another area, community or ethnic group. (3) It **extends** the witness of Christians from one area or locality to another forming a spiritual-physical link that can have an everlasting effect. (4) A new church can **conserve** members. New members, indifferent members and lazy members often can become totally involved in a new church. Many times, there does not seem to be enough "jobs" in an established church for all the members. (5) Breaking free of the "rut of tradition" can be another benefit. A new church can do things differently, they may not be better . . . but again, things done differently than at the "old, back-home church" may be better. At least, in a new church, it can be tried! It might only be having the morning worship service first rather than the Bible School. (6) Stewardship of money, time and talent must be developed to a greater extent. A new church will demand a better program of total **stewardship.** This demand will be upon those who choose to be members and upon those who will be assisting the new church to begin, such as a "Mother Church," or an evangelistic association. This is much like the demands of a new baby arriving into a home where the parents have only been concerned for themselves.

Perhaps the greatest reason of all for planting new churches is God's love and **our** love for the church in an age when so many are spiritually cold and indifferent. Timothy Dwight, an early president of Yale (1796) wrote in a great hymn about his love for the church:

I love Thy Kingdom, Lord
The house of thine abode;
The church our blest Redeemer saved
With His own precious blood.

I love thy church, O God,
Her walls before Thee stand.
Dear as the apple of Thine eye,
And graven on Thy Hand.

God unashamedly declared His love for the church in Ephesians 5:25-32:

Husbands, love your wives, just as Christ also loved the church and gave Himself up for her, that He might sanctify her, having cleansed her by the washing of water with the word, that He might present to Himself the church in all her glory, having no spot or wrinkle or any such thing; but that she should be holy and blameless. So husbands ought also to love their own wives as their own bodies. He who loves his own wife loves himself; for no one ever hated his own flesh, but nourishes and cherishes it, just as Christ also does the church, because we are members of His body. FOR THIS CAUSE A MAN SHALL LEAVE HIS FATHER AND MOTHER, AND SHALL CLEAVE TO HIS WIFE; AND THE TWO SHALL BECOME ONE FLESH. This mystery is great; but I am speaking with reference to Christ and the church.

Love for Christ's church, His body here on earth, will inspire us to establish His church wherever possible and wherever she is needed.

3

II

WHERE SHOULD NEW CHURCHES BE PLANTED?

 New churches should be started in any community, or city or area that lacks the Christian Church! If the city is of sufficient size, more than one church should be planted. I would hesitate to state the specific size of the city but perhaps for every three or four thousand in population a new church should be planted. Local conditions will govern this.

Distance should be a factor in new church planting. How near is the proposed new church location to another Christian Church? I know Christian Churches that thrive within a few miles of each other (one and one-half miles.) In the metropolitan area perhaps three to four miles will be as close as you would desire to locate churches. In such an area as the Greater Chicago Metropolitan area, we have tried to space out the new churches and then go back and fill in the spaces.

An apartment complex or "high-rise," or a mobile home court could lend itself to the establishment of a new church. Maybe the conventional church building would not be in order, but an apartment could be rented for services.

New subdivisions or new cities serve as admirable locations for new churches. We should be alert to the opportunities that are presented by the opening of a new subdivision, city, etc. and get in on the beginning of these new ventures of population growth.

There are many reasons why I believe the urban areas are high potential new church planting situations. In less than half of a century, America has ceased to be a rural nation! The United States is becoming highly urbanized. America is now a nation of great cities. Seventy percent of the people in the United States are living on ten percent of the land area and it is forecast that by the year 2000, eighty percent of the population will be surviving on ten percent of the land mass. Alexander Campbell foresaw this developing

4

problem in 1834. He was pointing to the cities when he said, "But the greatest need for evangelical, or what some call missionary labors, appears to exist in the eastern cities." John Mills of Chicago has said, "His cry has not been heard! America's vast cities, caught up in a population explosion, challenge us as never before!"

Also in the large cities, Christians will have an opportunity to evangelize the many ethnic and minority groups. Some of these groups are the Chinese, Japanese, Koreans, Germans, Russians, and others. The city or suburban church will have an opportunity to practice "observable love" to all men regardless of color, race, or creed.

A diligent study of the New Testament will reveal the church being established in the large centers of population. Jerusalem was a large urban area and must have been heavily populated because three thousand were baptized (Acts 2:38-47) on the day the Church began. Later we find additional preaching taking place and another five thousand believed (Acts 4:4) and no doubt were baptized. Within a short time, eight thousand have become members of the new Church (the first Church!) established in Jerusalem.

In fact, as you read the New Testament you will notice the Church being planted in city after city and flourishing. The letters of the Apostles give testimony to the growth of churches in the cities of the New Testament world. One is the Roman letter, written to the church in the city of Rome, the world's capitol, where sin and persecution were rampant. Paul's letters to the Corinthian church speak volumes of a church planted and growing in a citified atmosphere.

Donald McGavran in "How to Grow a Church" says that the apostolic church was a city church.

> We must recognize that the church grew in urban centers. The church grew strong in the great cities of the ancient world and must grow strong in the cities of North America. The New Testament tells, for the most part, about city churches. The church grew under city conditions. We can take courage from the fact that the church grew strong in the cities when it wasn't wealthy, and there were no church buildings. Christians met in homes. There was no printed New Testament. Followers of Christ were persecuted from time to time. Nevertheless, the living Lord led these early urban believers, and their churches multiplied.

The churches of the New Testament were urban churches! Let us plant new churches in the cities of this world!

Reprinted from How to Grow a Church (a Regal Book) by Donald A. McGavran and Win Arn by permission of G-L Publications. © Copyright 1973 by G—L Publications, Glendale, Calif. 91209.

III

AREA-WIDE SPONSORSHIP FOR A NEW CHURCH

 The church at Antioch of Syria in the thirteenth chapter of the Acts of The Apostles is a splendid example of area-wide leadership being provided for the purpose of planting new churches. This congregation was called by the Holy Spirit to "send out" the necessary leadership to evangelize (plant new churches). Saul (later known as Paul, Acts 13:9, 13) and Barnabas were set apart to the "work of the Holy Spirit." Later, Paul is found reporting to the Jerusalem congregation, Acts 15. It is obvious that the "Mother Church" of all the churches was concerned about the problems and trials as well as the growth of the new churches being planted by Paul and his co-workers in Asia and the continent of Europe. Leadership was being provided by men at the urging of the Holy Spirit.

Leadership and sponsorship for new churches today can come from a variety of sources. A mother congregation, a transplanted Christian family, an evangelistic association, a minister (evangelist), the co-operative effort of several congregations (not to be confused with the more permanent labors of an evangelistic association), or a Christian college may function in this capacity.

A mother congregation may be a very challenging source of sponsorship for a new church, providing strength to the "Mother Church" as well as the infant church. Planting a new church can be a richly rewarding experience for an established congregation. It can be the way for real growth, numerically as well as spiritually. It can, with proper leadership, and devotion to Christ, lead the rooted congregation to greater spiritual heights, as they assist sacrificially their "new-born babe" in the faith.

The dividing of assets, members and sometimes even sharing ministers can enhance the opportunities for growth in Christ-growth through witnessing in a new community or another city or growing by adding numerically to the

"Body of Christ" in both locations, new and old. "Mother" and "Child" will find it a very rewarding experience. Sponsoring a new church and mothering it will develop, as well as conserve, leadership.

Oftentimes a Christian family moving to an area not served by a church of their faith can take the initiative in planting a new church. It has been done many times. Our established congregations must see the necessity of preparing its families to move. American families are moving at least every four years on an average. The prepared Christian family can and will open their home to group Bible studies, worship services, Bible School classes, and this can lead into planning sessions for a new church. They can invite outside leadership evangelists, ministers, elders, teachers, etc.) to assist them. Aquila and Priscilla were forced by persecution to leave Rome. They came to Corinth and there they were found by Paul (Acts 18:1-11). Paul led them in the planting of a new church.

Many new churches are being planted by "evangelizing associations" (fellowships) of individuals and congregations. This method has many advantages for the following reasons.

1. In an "association" there are many people experienced in new church planting available for advice and encouragement. New Church planting from an evangelist's point of view can be lonely and depressing. He may also desire some answers to various questions or problems that may arise. An evangelistic association is a team effort or a pooling of knowledge and resources.

2. Experienced guidance can be given, free of charge, concerning the location, size, etc. of a building site, projected buildings, leadership, financing, etc. Ideas from men and women who have planted new churches will be given for the asking.

3. An evangelistic association does not expect to complete its mission when one or two churches are established and are functioning effectively. They will be planning future new churches in needy communities. The funds committed to planting new churches can be transferred to a new field of service.

4. Through an evangelistic association, small, medium and large churches and even individuals can participate together in the joy of planting new churches. Substantial sums can be contributed.

5. Churches and individuals in another area will more readily participate in the planting of churches through an evangelistic association. They will know that responsible and dedicated leadership will be supplied to the new church planting effort.

Ministers of nearby churches have often been able to provide leadership for a new church. What a blessing it is to an individual to be able to see beyond the borders of his particular city or area and to visualize the opportunity to evangelize in another city, area or ethnic group by planting a new church. Ministers should and can enlist and challenge their respective elders, deacons, Bible School teachers and the congregation to lead out in a venture of faith. How rewarding it can be to advocate "church growth" at the expense of "congregational development" yet a "planned" and "supported" new church will bring congregational growth in many areas. The inspired leadership of a dedicated "church planting" minister can revolutionize his congregation and the communities in which the "old" and the "new" thrive. Christian colleges and seminaries should inspire and challenge their students and graduates to lead out in "new church evangelism." Ministerial students must be taught to conserve converts by planting new churches in their respective communities. The average Christian seems to lose interest after a time, if he must drive over ten minutes to worship and often refuses to participate in religious activities. Furthermore Christians do not bring their friends and neighbors to services or evangelize them when they are separated by too much distance from the house of worship. The evangelistically inclined minister will recognize the value of establishing more "Spiritual Beachheads" (new churches) for Christ, his Lord.

The co-operative efforts of several congregations (not to be confused with the more permanent labors of an evangelistic association) can successfully establish a new church or churches.   A combined sharing of members, contributions of members, pooling their leadership ability and know-how, and funds, will make it possible for them to double the number of churches in their city or metropolitan area. Perhaps that black community or other ethnic area would best be evangelized by the combined efforts of a number of Christ-oriented congregations? Too often we have applied the "Great Commission" (Matthew 28:18-20; Mark 16:14-16; Luke 24:44-49; Acts 1:8) to foreign missions and have forgotten lost souls in the nearby city or community.

In some areas the Christian colleges have furnished leadership for the establishment of new churches. This is an excellent method but each church planted should be looked upon as a "long-term" project and planned and assisted in that manner. "Short-term" leadership and sponsorship can be very detrimental to the growth of an infant congregation. A college planned and sponsored new congregation can supply an outlet of service for the student body as well as for the faculty who may not be preaching. It will give the ministerial students an opportunity to function effectively under the guidance of the experienced faculty members. It will give all college-related personnel an opportunity and the privilege of sharing their faith in Christ with those outside of Christ.

Concerned and dedicated churches hundreds of miles from the site of the new church planting can lend their assistance and make possible leadership through their support of the efforts of an evangelistic association or an evangelist. The First Christian Church of Clinton, Ill. (Winston Zastrow, senior minister) has taken me as their minister (living-link missionary) of evangelism to the greater Chicago Metropolitan area. I also serve and report to the Chicago District Evangelistic Association as evangelist-at-large. The First Christian Church of Greenville, Illinois sponsored for many years the efforts of the Richard Thayer family in planting new churches in the difficult mission field of the New England States. Many other churches in Southern

Illinois and Southern Indiana also have a vital interest in "new church evangelism" in the greater Chicago Metropolitan area. They have contributed money and members. What has been said about interest in the Chicago area by many downstate churches has been repeated throughout the nation by many churches as they send members and support to unchurched areas.

It is quite evident to me that "area-wide sponsorship" is necessary and Scriptural if new churches are to be planted in any city, community or area.

For preliminary guidelines that will aid in "Mothering" a new church, see page 96.

IV

BEGINNING WITH A NUCLEUS FOR A NEW CHURCH

A number of methods or sources for recruiting a nucleus have been used and proven successful when a new church has been organized. They are as follows:

1. Members and leadership families are recruited from nearby concerned and sponsoring churches. This has proven to be the best source for a new church nucleus. These devoted Christians should be ready and able to lead out in a spirit-filled venture for Christ. These can be recruited by inspirational evangelistic challenges from the pulpit, in the Bible School classes, through the church newsletter and by an example-setting leadership. A special day for these "new church recruits" may be held by the sponsoring churches.

2. The Christians' friends and relatives are the next best source of recruitment. This refers particularly to the recruit nucleus. They can be enlisted and can be converted for the cause of Christ. Sometimes this is just the challenge that can reach and soften the heart of some friend or relative. It may also harden the heart because they have never walked in faith.

3. The Bible School enrollment records of the sponsoring churches should be examined carefully. They can lead to many worthwhile contacts. If the Bible School teachers in the new church's Bible School will keep accurate records and pursue leads offered in this manner, the nucleus will be blessed by many additions. Many authorities have declared this to be the best source of prospects for any church.

4. As news of the planned new church circulates among sister churches, many of them will write concerning former members who are located in areas of the proposed new church. Announcements concerning the new church to brotherhood papers and newletters should elicit a desired response from their readers.

10

5. Silent roll call cards (attendance cards) can be used each Sunday by members and the visitors. If this worthwhile practice is instituted at the beginning of the infant congregation it will become a very good habit. Experience has proven this to be a rich source of prospects. Also the "attendance cards" will enable the minister and the elders to keep records on the attendance of the members. Sample copies of attendance cards are to be found on page 14.

6. Newcomers to the community are an excellent source of members and will often be challenged to form the nucleus for a new church, especially younger couples and couples who have raised their children. These newcomers can be found by subscribing to the local Welcome Wagon or some similar organization. Such organizations may be found in the "Yellow Pages" of the local telephone directory or by contacting the local Chamber of Commerce. Friendly churches in the community will often give a new church valuable leads toward obtaining lists of prospects. In some communities, the local Chamber of Commerce compiles a list of newcomers for businesses, etc. Once the new church is established, the Chamber of Commerce will be very co-operative. The members and the friends of the new church can observe the presence of moving vans in the immediate neighborhood and call on their new neighbors in the name of their church. These newcomers to the neighborhood should also be added to the church's prospect list. Follow-up letters from the congregation welcoming the newcomers to the community, telephone calls reinforcing the letters and also screening the newcomers as to the value of a personal call, will be helpful in contacting the newcomer. A sample of a letter that could be sent to the newcomers is on page 15. Some of the Utilities will be willing to give the church a list of new subscribers to their services. These names should be followed up in the same manner as those on the Welcome Wagon and Chamber of Commerce lists.

7. Prospects can be found through the use of advertising in the daily newspapers, paid ads and free publicity. Free publicity can be secured by submitting write-ups of important events that are happening in the life of your church. Such events as: special programs (use names of persons); special meetings; special days; special speakers; special series of sermons; election of officers; ordination of elders and deacons; special visitors; record attendances; dedications; and the calling of a minister, etc. are accepted by most newspapers. Most metropolitan communities have "free circulars," these are distributed from door-to-door. Almost everybody reads the want-ads. Ads in free circulars have proven to be very effective and inexpensive. Early contacts should be made with the local radio and TV stations. Information can be secured from them as to what type of free advertising they will accept. Many times the minister will be asked to contribute devotions and prayers. This is excellent free promotion for the church. Not to be forgotten are the religious journals of the Brotherhood and the College and Seminary newsletters of the

minister-evangelist. These journals and newsletters are always ready to print brotherhood news and the activities of their alumni.

8. After the congregation has been established, a religious census or house-to-house survey can be conducted. For further information turn to the chapter on "New Church Evangelism."

9. A telephone survey can be very effective if well-organized and the callers are trained. Special telephone books can be secured for this purpose but they are expensive. See your phone company. Some of the older, more mature ladies can prepare phone-calling lists in the vicinity of the church building or the meeting place. They will also make excellent callers. Follow-up letters and personal calls will be in order for any prospect uncovered.

10. Door-to-door visitation, not to be confused with "surveying" or "canvassing" or a "religious census," has proven to be very effective. Getting acquainted with the neighborhood, introducing yourself, and sharing your faith, and inviting the neighbor to the services of the congregation, can be very rewarding and fruitful.

11. Institutional visitation . . . calling in hospitals, nursing homes (homes for the elderly and infirm), child-care centers, and retirement centers, etc. will harvest souls for Christ. Some new churches have been filled by such concerned visitation and follow-up. By follow-up, I mean calling on the friends and relatives that have been contacted in this way. Of course, calls should be made on hospital patients after they have returned home.

12. A daily Vacation Bible School is always a vital source for contacts when planting a new church. There are many ways in which Vacation Bible Schools can be held by a congregation meeting in rented quarters. Often the same building being used by the new church can be rented for a week, for evenings or for daytime use. Vacation Bible School can be held in the homes of the members or even in the backyards. The important thing is have a well-planned school. Be sure and obtain the vital information concerning the address, name, age, grade and religious background of the pupil. This vital information will be used to reach the pupil and parents for Christ and His church.

13. "Bible and Fun Clubs" held on Saturdays or weekday evenings after school can advertise to the community and to the parents the love and the concern of the new church for the youth of the community. These need not be large to be effective. They can be held in various locations.

14. Families in need are reachable for Christ. The members of the church should always be alert to the opportunities to assist families and individuals that are in need. Jesus had much to say about this in Matthew 25:31-46. It is not enough to be concerned about the spiritual nature of man, man's physical needs must also be met. Often meeting these needs can be the means of leading him to Christ.

15. Weddings, newlyweds, new parents, and deaths provide opportunities in which many people are more open to spiritual assistance. Your interest and concern can touch them deeply and in loving you they will love your Saviour. Many people are more reachable for Christ in these times than at any other time. Even a contact from an announcement in the daily newspaper may be of value in reaching the joyous or distressed person, which ever may be the case, for Christ.

16. Too much cannot be said about the value of "Bible study" sessions in homes and in other buildings. One good leader, teaching and leading a discussion of the Bible, can bring many people to acknowledge their need for Christ's redeeming power. These can be held during the day, or in the evenings. Perhaps the "coffee hour" in the neighborhood can be an hour devoted to Bible study and prayer? The emphasis must be upon Bible study and prayer and not upon psychoanalysis, confession of sins and the sharing of emotional upheavals. The Gospel is the power of God unto salvation (Romans 1:15-17; I Corinthians 1:17-25).

The structure of the nucleus may be determined in two parts, the **permanent** members and the **supportive** members. The latter may be concerned Christians from sister churches who are willing to lend their services on a temporary basis. They will assist in the following manner: as pianist, teacher, preacher, etc. The **permanent** members of the nucleus will of course be the charter members and will fill such necessary offices as:

1. Financial secretary
2. Treasurer
3. Historian
4. Corresponding secretary
5. Church clerk
6. Secretary
7. Bible School co-ordinator (superintendent)
8. Nursery chairman
9. Communion chairman
10. Usher and welcome chairman
11. Publicity chairman
12. Equipment chairman
13. Worship chairman

Please see pages 25-27 for a "Job Description" of the above-mentioned offices or officers. The **permanent** members should always serve in every capacity whenever possible; **supportive** members will only serve temporarily.

Included in this chapter is an outline of "suggested steps toward organizing a church." Please see page 16. In the planning sessions with the nucleus, these "steps" are to be discussed and should be followed as closely as possible. Perhaps there will be some revising to apply to various situations.

Too much cannot be said at this point as to the blessings of a sizeable membership in the beginning and a well-trained and dedicated leadership. Experience has proven these two factors can contribute much to rapid and proper growth, numerically and spiritually.

ATTENDANCE CARD

Name ....

Street Address ....

City ....

Date .... ( )a.m. ( )p.m.

   ( ) Child: 12 years or under

   ( ) Youth: 12 to 21 years

   ( ) Adult: 22 and older

( ) Member of this congregation?

     Member of what church? ....

....

( ) Interested in becoming a Christian.

( ) Interested in placing membership here.

( ) Would like the preacher to call.

( ) Would like a box of offering envelopes.

ATTENDANCE CARD   ( ) AM   ( ) PM

DATE_____

    Miss

NAME Mrs._____PHONE_____

    Mr.

ADDRESS_____

_____ZIP_____

CHURCH MEMBERSHIP: ( ) Here   ( ) No Membership
( ) Child to age 12   ( ) Youth 13-21   ( ) Adult

( ) I am a member of _____Church.
( ) I am interested in becoming a Christian.
( ) I am interested in placing my membership here.
( ) I am interested in having the minister to call.
( ) I wish to receive offering envelopes.

14

CHURCH LETTERHEAD

Dear New Neighbor:

May we welcome you to our delightful community.

One of the vital factors in making our community a wonderful place to live are the churches!

We would be very happy to have you visit us and worship with us. Our church is a friendly neighborhood church.

Soon, our minister or one of the members will call on you and give you a personal welcome to our neighborhood. A personal invitation will also be extended to you to attend our inspirational services. Our program for the WHOLE family will also be explained.

May God bless you in your new residence and your family.

A Concerned Church,

P.S. Enclosed find a brochure describing our congregation.

SOME SUGGESTED STEPS TOWARD ORGANIZING A CHURCH . . . .

(1) Planning a new congregation
Mother church, evangelistic association
Minister, evangelist, leader
Sister churches
Christians, prospects
Advertising
Name
Meeting place
Starting date and program
Treasurer, secretary

(2) Infant church (one to six months)
Sunday services
Minister, evangelist
Congregational meetings
Congregational chairman
Canvassing
Visitation
At least ten percent for missions
Charter membership
Non-profit state incorporation
Apply for association membership
Bible School superintendent
Other church officers

(3) New Church—(six months to two years)
Leadership committee selected
Adopt budget
Adopt goals
Apply to Assn. for ministerial help
Part-time minister
Advisor—evangelist-at-large
By-laws
Departments

(4) New church (two years)
Elect elders and deacons
Full-time minister
Annual business meeting
Goals re-examined
Site secured
Building plans underway
Graded Bible School
Primary Church services

Departments	Leadership committee
Finance	selected men
Worship	Selected by Church
Education	Advisor-evangelist
Building and site	minister
Evangelism	Reports to congregation
Ministerial	Members of the church

V
THE PLANNING SESSIONS FOR A NEW CHURCH

 Once the hard core of prospective members, **permanent** members, the nucleus, has been found, planning sessions can be held. The nucleus can be composed of two or three families or many families. The more families available for the nucleus and especially leadership families, the more satisfactory will be the beginning of the new congregation.

The planning sessions can be held in a home, a sister church, a rented hall, etc. These should be under the leadership of an organizing evangelist, minister or an experienced church leader.

The nearby churches, Brotherhood churches, should be notified of the "planning sessions" and their leaders invited to attend the sessions. Perhaps meetings could be arranged with the near-by church leaders prior to the announcing of "planning sessions" for the new church. It may be possible to enlist their assistance and to lean upon them for guidance. This will be needed and so will their best wishes and prayers.

In preparation for the planning sessions each family should have a copy of this book. Each chapter could be studied prior to or during the planning sessions. It would also be well to have on hand a supply of the forms and materials suggested in this book.

Open the sessions with devotions by a neighboring preacher or church leader if possible. Following devotions, discussion will be held as to "why a new congregation" and as to who will be sponsoring it, if it is to have a sponsor.

A volunteer secretary will be recruited. Detailed minutes should be taken of all "planning sessions." These will be invaluable for reference and will be preserved for their historical value. If a photograph can be taken of each session this too would be of much interest in later years.

Early in the first meeting of the planning sessions, the form "Some Suggested Steps Toward Organizing a New Church" should be introduced. This form can be found on page 16. A copy of this form should be in the hands of each interested person at the planning session. The step-by-step procedure of this form will be of great value in planning the agenda for the planning sessions.

All those present for the "planning session or sessions" should be given a voice.

As progress is made in the planning sessions, maybe even at the first session, questions will arise as to a name for the new church. Someone will want to know, "Where shall we meet?" Another may ask, "When will we begin and what will the program be?"

These are all good questions and the leader will be ready with the answers! Or at least, he will be able to assist the nucleus in arriving at some answers. How about a name? There are many Scriptural names available. Many churches are named not only after Christ, but according to the location in which they may be meeting. Sometimes in the early life stages of the embryo congregation, one name is chosen, and later another, more suitable, is selected. Whatever name the congregation-to-be decides upon, it should be done by ballot.

Next will be the ever present thought, "Where can we meet for Sunday services?" The leader can point out that often public schools are available and can be rented (occasionally, there is no charge) for Sunday services. In many areas, various halls can be rented, such as: the Odd Fellows' Hall, the Moose Lodge Hall, a Y.M.C.A. or Y.W.C.A. building (the gym and other rooms), the American Legion building, a Union Hall, a Seventh Day Adventist Church building, etc. As a rule, the Seventh Day Adventist Church building would be the best facility because of its "churchy" atmosphere. A committee of those living in the locality of where the church is to be planted should be appointed by the chairman (leader) to seek this meeting place. The authorities will be more in sympathy with the local citizenry.

The organizing evangelist (leader) must work closely with the above committee as well as with other committees.

At another planning session, second or third, the question will again arise, "When will we begin to meet as a formal congregation" (beginning date for worship services and Sunday School)? After much discussion, the leader will suggest that those interested in being a member, a permanent member, shall fill out an affirmation of interest form. Included is a form on page 20 that is very useful in securing a decision and other needed information. Much of the information included on this form is very vital to organizing a new church.

Upon the examination of the affirmation form and if there is an adequate number to organize a new church, the decision can be made as to when the new church can begin formally. The proposed new congregation should vote on this issue.

The "planning sessions" may be held for about three to six months prior to the actual formal worship services and the signing of the charter. They should be held once a week or at least every other week. Some of the reasons for so many planning sessions are as follows: fellowship (getting acquainted), teaching and inspiration, observation and developing of leadership, planning and organizing, etc.

As the "planning sessions" continue it will be well to refer to the "Planning Session Check List" for guidelines in preparing for the formal beginning of the new church. This form is found on page 21.

AFFIRMATION OF INTEREST

☐I am interested in a new church in this area and will be a member of it.

Name _____

_____

       Address   **Zip Code**

_____

                                            Phone

My present membership (church) is at:

_____

My activities in church work and Bible School have been as follows:

☐Teacher in Bible School
   Please list class, age group, etc.

_____

☐Elder

☐Deacon

☐Pianist

☐Organist

☐Choir

☐Soloist

☐Choir director

☐Typist

☐Operated mimeograph

☐Boy Scouts

☐Youth sponsor

☐Bible School officer

Please list other activities you have participated in that are not mentioned.

Please list your children:

Name	Age	School grade	Baptized

PLANNING SESSIONS' CHECK LIST

Check off

1. _____ Devotions and explanation of last meeting.

2. _____ Discussion and vote on formal organization (by ballot).

3. _____ Discussion and decision concerning a place to meet on Sundays.

4. _____ Select a name for the new church.

5. _____ Select or elect officers, such as: Treasurer, Financial Secretary, Church Clerk, Bible School Co-ordinator, Teachers, Bible School Secretary, Trustees or directors, Various Chairmen of Committees (Nursery, Communion, Welcome and Ushering, Publicity, Equipment and Worship) Corresponding Secretary, Secretary and Historian.

6. _____ Bible School supplies for classes:

Nursery, Ages 1, 2, 3   Niners, Grade nine.
Preschool, Ages 4 and 5.   Senior Hi, Grades ten, eleven
Primary, Grades one and two.   and twelve.
Junior, Grades three and four.   College
Middler, Grades five and six.   Adult
Junior Hi, Grades seven and eight.

7. _____ Supply preacher (part-time).

8. _____ Discussion of Incorporation, Not-for-profit, State or County.

9. _____ Equipment needed, see check list of equipment.

10. _____ Selection or election of trustees.

11. _____ Brochures, for publicity, for canvassing, for use in bulletins.

12. _____ Hours for worship, Bible School, Evening Services, Bible Study, etc.

13. _____ Programs for Worship and Bible School.

14. _____ Youth Work, Sponsors, etc.

15. _____ Publicity, Newspaper, Radio, Religious journals, First Day Services, etc.

16. _____ Building Supervisor and Equipment Management.

17. _____ The Charter and Membership.

18. _____ Additional items not mentioned:

19. Devotions for next meeting, to be assigned.

20. Date and place of next "Planning Session" or business meeting.

VI
CONGREGATIONAL LEADERSHIP FOR A NEW CHURCH

In order that the new church may function properly, organization will be needed. Much of the organizing will be done at the "planning sessions" prior to the formal opening of the church's charter. The Apostle Paul admonishes us that "Everything must be done in a proper and orderly way" (I Corinthians 14:40 TEV).

The importance of dedicated, spiritual, courageous congregational leadership cannot be stressed enough. Many of the churches have printed the following quotation in their newsletters: "WHAT MAKES A GREAT CHURCH? It's ... not big budgets, but big hearts; not money received, but the services rendered; not tall buildings, but lofty visions; not record-breaking attendance but God's presence; not frantic motions, but dedicated action; not soft seats and bright lights, but courageous leadership and true followers; not loud talking, but quiet doing; not members in beautiful clothes, but members living godly lives; not preachers telling it their way, but teachers stressing the truth and living thereby; not actions in the past, but things being done **NOW**."

An examination of successful new churches will indicate there was strong, spiritual leadership on the part of the man in the pew and the man in the pulpit. Growing new churches with adequate planning never just happens. Where it exists, it means there is a corps of leaders including the preacher-evangelist, who dedicate themselves to making church planning succeed. A thriving working new church program means:

—The church must be **mobilized** for planning.

—The church must be **enlisted** to carry out its plans.

—The church must be **informed** of the plans.

—The church must be **committed** to provide the necessary spiritual life, talent and resources.

Medford Jones says, "Leadership in the church was once thought of in the terms of holding an office or having a certain position. It was equated with

22

authority, viewed as a matter of directing other people, and considered to reside in specific persons."

"A more dynamic view of leadership is emerging; according to the newer understanding, leadership is a function that can and should be shared by all the members of a group.

A person is serving as a leader whenever he helps the group to:
1. Realize, understand, and remember what its purpose is.
2. Set and agree upon goals that will aid the fulfillment of that purpose.
3. Work together effectively as a team.
4. Find ways and marshal resources to accomplish its goals and purposes."

The list of leaders (officers) to be elected and their jobs are given in the "Job Description" form on pages 25-27. When the new church is being organized it is the best policy to elect leaders for a year or for the balance of the calendar year.

Usually elders and deacons are not elected until the congregation is about two years old, although there have been exceptions to this rule. Waiting two years, while the men serve in various leadership capacities, will give the men an opportunity to prove themselves to the new church. To serve as an elder or a deacon does not require election and ordination to that office. Before a man is elected to the high office of elder or deacon the congregation should be given the opportunity to observe him in action and to compare him with the Scriptural qualifications as listed in Acts 6:1-6; I Timothy 3:1-7, 8-13; II Timothy 2:20-26; Titus 1:5-9, 2:1-6; and I Peter 5:1-4. A form that can be used in the selection or election of elders and deacons is to be found on page 87.

In the early stages of the embryo congregation the business is conducted by congregational meetings and a congregational chairman is selected by the congregation. Sometimes the organizing evangelist will lead these congregational meetings.

After about six months and no later than a year, the church will select a "leadership committee." This committee can be composed of the outstanding, spiritual leaders of the church. The "leadership committee" will select a chairman and a secretary. These are not to be confused with the chairman of the congregation and the church clerk or church secretary. The minister-evangelist should serve on this committee in an ex-officio manner. Please see page 32 for Leadership Guidelines form.

Under the congregational leadership, comes the important question, "Who will preach for this congregation?" Often there are many avenues open, such as: the organizing evangelist, a Christian college professor, a preaching church leader, a former preacher-minister now employed in another vocation, the minister of a near-by church (the hours of service can be staggered), a Christian college student, etc. The best man available should be chosen for the part-time ministry of this new church.

In the calling of a full-time evangelist or minister, the utmost caution must be exercised. **Here is one of the most important steps** to be taken by a new congregation. Much will depend upon the leadership quality of the minister. Congregational growth, spiritually and numerically, will hinge upon the mature and spiritual nature of the man called. His must essentially be an "equipping ministry," Ephesians 4:11-16. Yet, the minister must lead out in example as well as with the Word. He must be expected to lead by being "apt to call" in the homes of the congregation and prospects. With his leadership ability, the minister will teach others "how to call, how to teach, how to give generously, etc."

It is my considered and experienced opinion that guidance in the selection of a full-time minister must be sought by the congregation. This guidance can be found in counseling with nearby ministers and church leadership, the evangelistic association involved (if one is involved), a nearby Christian college, etc. References and a resume must be required of an applicant. A suggested reference questionnaire is included on pages 28-29. The resume must include such items as: schooling, ministries, family information, accomplishments, strengths and dislikes in ministering to a congregation, age, future plans, etc. A picture must accompany the resume. A questionnaire to be used in assisting the applicant prepare a resume is to be found on pages 33-34. After the pulpit committee, selected by the leadership committee or the congregation or elders and deacons, examines the resume and obtains the necessary references, at least eight, they can interview the applicant and hear him deliver a sermon at his home church. This procedure can be followed for several applicants but the decision must be narrowed to one applicant and he can be asked to preach a trial sermon and the congregation is asked for a decision. The applicant must have a large majority of the vote (eighty percent?) before he can be called.

If a supporting evangelistic association or "Mother" church is involved, then full consideration must be given to their desires and recommendations.

The congregation is to have the final opportunity to accept or reject the ministerial candidate.

After the church has been functioning for a period of time, departments can be organized. One person can lead and serve as the department head until more can be enlisted. The Church Department chart on page 30 was first developed by Dr. Paul Benjamin, Director of the National Church Growth Research Center of Washington, D.C.

A knowledgeable leadership will adopt well-thought-out goals—goals that will be workable and realistic, goals that are attainable. These will be goals that pertain to growth, spiritually and numerically.

Not to be neglected in the organized life of the infant church is the planned Sunday worship services, both morning and evening. The first planning and organizing will be done in the "planning sessions" but as time goes by it will be well to review the progress and accomplishments of these services. Are they understandable, are they workable, are they spiritual, do the worship services lead the participants closer to God? A suggested Sunday worship program for a new church is included on page 31.

JOB DESCRIPTIONS
The Financial Secretary

1. Count the offerings and keep an accurate record of all monies received.
2. Reports are to be given to individual contributors upon request. An annual report shall be given to each contributor by the 15th of January of each year.
3. Deposit all monies in the bank as soon as possible. Deposit slip is to be given to the treasurer at once. To serve as assistant Treasurer.
4. Give a monthly report of monies received and deposited.
5. Serve on the Finance Committee if one is functioning.

The Treasurer

1. Receive the deposit slips from the Financial Secretary.
2. Keep accurate books and submit them for auditing.
3. Give monthly reports to the congregation.   Submit an annual report by the 15th of January of each year.
4. Pay all bills that have been approved by the proper committees, leadership committee, elders and deacons or the congregation.
5. Order and distribute offering envelopes (Financial Secretary could do this).
6. Serve on the Finance Committee if one is functioning.

Historian

1. Receive and keep all papers, pictures, bulletins, etc. that will record the historical events and growth of the congregation.
2. Catalogue the above material.
3. Be alert to every opportunity to record events and facts that may be of value in later years.

Corresponding Secretary

1. Mail out Sunday bulletins to absentees and prospective members.
2. Mail sick cards, birthday greetings, anniversary cards and sympathy cards.
3. Send out "Welcome Visitor" letters or cards.
4. Send reports of additions, etc. to interested religious journals.

Church Clerk

1. Record baptisms and transfer of memberships and issue certificates.
2. Send change of membership letters and keep accurate records of membership.
3. Keep minutes of congregational meetings and record treasurer's reports.
4. Keep worship and Sunday school attendance records.

Secretary

1. Prepare and mimeograph the Sunday Bulletin.
2. Keep canvassing records and records of new prospects.
3. Co-ordinate telephone programs.

Bible School Co-ordinator

1. Order supplies.
2. Work with teachers and assistant teachers toward regularity and provide replacement teachers.
3. Designate person or persons to keep adequate records (attendance and offerings).
4. Recruit teachers from those who are immersed believers in Christ.
5. Preside and (or) arrange for opening services (if any) or closing services (if any) and special days in the Sunday School.
6. Work towards a better School and assist the teachers at all times.

Nursery Chairperson

1. Co-ordinate the efforts of nursery volunteers.
2. Supply information of volunteers to church secretary.
3. Maintain presentable nursery services for the church.
4. Be alert to all problems and possibilities in nursery care and seek assistance.
5. Be in charge of the nursery supplies.

Communion Chairperson

1. Co-ordinate the efforts of communion preparation volunteers.
2. Supply the information of volunteers to the church secretary.
3. Supervise the care of linens, etc.
4. Procure materials as they are needed for communion preparation.

Welcome and Usher Chairperson

1. Enlist others to serve as ushers.
2. Arrange a schedule of ushers.
3. Instruct ushers as to the proper ventilation, when and where to seat people, etc.
4. Distribute Sunday bulletins.
5. Promote a warm friendly atmosphere among the congregation and the visitors.
6. Co-ordinate the efforts of the men serving communion and receiving the offering. After the Leadership Committee is selected, the chairman can assume this responsibility if he so desires.

Publicity Chairperson

1. Bring to the attention of both the church and the community; the teachings, the programs, the life, the functions and special meetings of the church.
2. Provide newspaper publicity or other forms of publicity as needed.
3. Provide pictures for church periodicals and local newspapers.
4. Provide news for the church bulletin.

Equipment Chairperson

1. Co-ordinate the placing of chairs and other equipment on Sundays.
2. Seek volunteers to assist in the above matter.
3. Assume responsibility for hymnbooks, etc. (all equipment while church is meeting in rented quarters).

Worship Chairperson

1. Assume responsibility for special music (if possible.)
2. Appeal for flowers for the worship service (arrange for disposal, too).
3. Be alert for opportunities to improve the worship services. This is to be co-ordinated with the minister.

RESOLUTIONS FOR CHURCH WORKERS

I will accept my office believing God needs me right there.
I will do my best—and not my "excuse best!"
I will be loyal and faithful to the worship services.
I will learn the "how" of my office and not remain ignorant of its functions.
I will spend some time in prayer and Bible study each day.
I will remember that my church will be judged by my actions and will seek to make my daily life count for much.
I will strengthen the hand of my preacher and the leaders of my church.
I will try to win the lost to Christ and be friendly to them and the whole church.
I will, above all, try to know God's will and follow it.

—Copied—

Dear

The above mentioned has expressed an interest in "new church" work in the Chicago area. Your name has been suggested as a reference and we will appreciate it very much if you will fill out this form and return it as soon as possible. Thank you for responding to our request.

Length and Nature of Relationship to the Applicant:
1. How long have you known the applicant?

☐less than one year ☐one to three years ☐over three years
2. In what capacity?

Spiritual and Moral Stature
3. Do you have any reservations about the applicant's commitment to Christ and faithfulness to the Word of God?

☐none whatsoever ☐some doubt ☐undecided.

Please explain your response:

4. What is your estimation of this applicant's moral character?
☐above reproach ☐some doubt ☐questionable.

Please explain your response:

Assumption of Responsibilities
5. How would you rate this applicant's ability to assume personal and professional responsibilities?

☐very dependable ☐dependable ☐not dependable
6. How well does this applicant organize and manage his ministerial functions and duties?

☐outstanding ☐above average ☐average ☐below average

Interpersonal Relationships
7. How would you describe the applicant's ability to relate and work with others?

☐exceptionally effective ☐effective ☐less than effective

Please comment:

8. How would you describe this applicant's physical appearance?

☐neat/well groomed ☐average/clean ☐below average/careless

9. What is your estimation of this applicant's ability to motivate and facilitate spiritual growth in others?

☐outstanding ☐good ☐adequate ☐ineffective

10. What age groups does the applicant work with effectively?

☐mature adults ☐young adults ☐youth ☐children

11. What do you perceive as this applicant's greatest asset?

12. What do you perceive as his greatest liability?

Minister's Wife

13. Is this applicant's wife an asset to his ministry?

☐yes ☐no

Please comment:

14. Is the household kept neat and well organized? ☐yes ☐no.

Please comment:

Final Summary

15. Do you have any reservations about recommending this person as a minister-evangelist for a new church?

Please comment:

Signed _____

Position _____

(All answers will be kept confidential,)

ORGANIZATIONAL CHART FOR
A FUNCTIONAL CHURCH

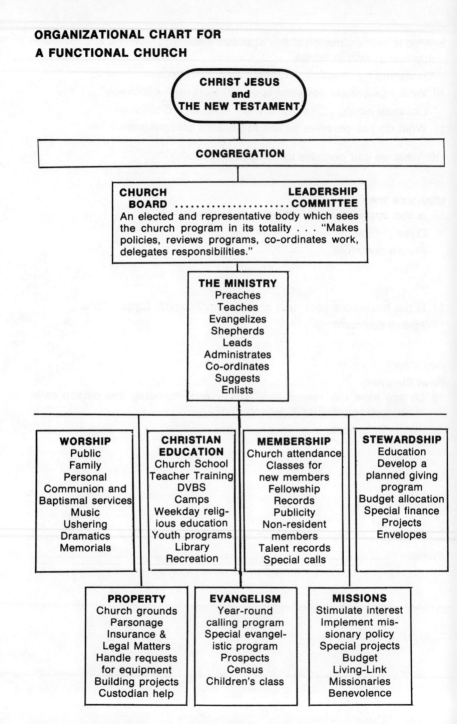

CHRIST JESUS
and
THE NEW TESTAMENT

CONGREGATION

CHURCH BOARD .... **LEADERSHIP COMMITTEE**
An elected and representative body which sees the church program in its totality . . . "Makes policies, reviews programs, co-ordinates work, delegates responsibilities."

THE MINISTRY
Preaches
Teaches
Evangelizes
Shepherds
Leads
Administrates
Co-ordinates
Suggests
Enlists

WORSHIP
Public
Family
Personal
Communion and
Baptismal services
Music
Ushering
Dramatics
Memorials

CHRISTIAN EDUCATION
Church School
Teacher Training
DVBS
Camps
Weekday relig-
ious education
Youth programs
Library
Recreation

MEMBERSHIP
Church attendance
Classes for
new members
Fellowship
Records
Publicity
Non-resident
members
Talent records
Special calls

STEWARDSHIP
Education
Develop a
planned giving
program
Budget allocation
Special finance
Projects
Envelopes

PROPERTY
Church grounds
Parsonage
Insurance &
Legal Matters
Handle requests
for equipment
Building projects
Custodian help

EVANGELISM
Year-round
calling program
Special evangel-
istic program
Prospects
Census
Children's class

MISSIONS
Stimulate interest
Implement mis-
sionary policy
Special projects
Budget
Living-Link
Missionaries
Benevolence

Name
Address
City and Phone

Lord's Day   Date

WORSHIP IN PRAISE

The Prelude
Call to Worship   Matt. 1:18-25
Hymn of Praise
Welcome and Announcements
Silent Roll-Call Cards Signed
Hymn of Prayer
Prayer

WORSHIP IN COMMUNION

Hymn of Communion
Communion Meditation
     Partaking individually of the bread and the cup as they are passed.
Offering

WORSHIP IN RENEWAL

Message
Hymn of Decision
Benediction
Closing Chorus

"Learn as if you were to live forever; live as if you were to die tomorrow."

31

GUIDELINES FOR THE LEADERSHIP COMMITTEE
(Steering Committee)

1. Act as liaison between the minister-evangelist and the new congregation.
2. Assume responsibilities delegated to them by the congregation. Such as:
   a. Everyday business affairs of the congregation.
   b. Provide leadership for Bible School, worship, prayer meetings, etc.
   c. Develop leadership within the congregation.
   d. Provide leadership in evangelism, such as: calling and visitation or study sessions.
   e. Offer spiritual guidance for the congregation.
3. Meet in a planned business session at least once a month. Some suggestions:
   a. Meet on a day other than Sunday.
   b. Elect a chairman, assistant chairman and secretary.
   c. Appoint committees for special opportunities.
   d. All business done in an orderly manner.
   e. Open with prayer and devotions and close with prayer.
4. Meet with the minister-evangelist for discussion, evaluations, devotions, etc. at least once a month and more often would be better. Your minister-evangelist needs your fellowship, prayers and encouragement.
5. Recognize responsibility toward the "Mothering church," the evangelistic association, etc. that may be sponsoring the new church.
6. In case of radical departure from the normal business, such as: (a) problems with the minister-evangelist) (b) seeking and purchasing a building site; (c) a desire to ask their minister-evangelist to resign; (d) divisions within the congregation, etc., guidance should be sought from the "Mothering church," the evangelistic association, etc.
7. Be alert to every possibility to improve the spiritual life of the new church.
8. Be aware of the physical requirements and problems within the congregation.
9. Be on the watch for any attempt to dilute the Word of God as it is being taught and preached.
10. Maintain good relationships with the community-at-large, yet, do not permit God's truth to be compromised.
11. The minister-evangelist will be a non-voting member of the Leadership Committee.
12. The Leadership Committee will report to the congregation in its regular meetings and seek guidance from the congregation.
13. It will be well for the Leadership Committee to initiate special study classes. Such as: (a) What It Means to be a Christian) (b) How to Become a Christian; (c) Stewardship; (d) Leadership; (e) The Church; (f) Prayer Life; (g) the Worship Life of the Church; (h) Evangelism, etc. These special classes could be taught by a minister or an elder or college professor.

A QUESTIONNAIRE FOR RESUME INFORMATION AND PERSONAL EVALUATION MATERIAL FOR MINISTER/EVANGELIST APPLICANTS ..

1. Name _____ Age _____

2. Address _____

3. Wife's Name _____ How many children?_____

4. Ages of children _____

5. From which college/seminary did you graduate?_____

6. What degree(s) do you hold?_____

7. What is your present location and area of service?

8. Are you in good health? _____ Are there any physical disabilities which might impair your ability to conduct an active ministry?

9. Does your wife cooperate well with you in your work as minister? _____

10. Do you get along well with others? _____

11. Do you consider yourself to be an evangelistic type minister? _____

12. MATTERS OF FAITH (Please use extra sheet or back of this page to answer):
    a. How do you feel about the "tongues" issue?
    b. Do you believe there is such a place as Hell?
    c. Explain your belief as to the inspiration and authority of the Scriptures.
    d. Do you believe in the virgin birth and bodily resurrection of our Lord?
    e. Do you hold any beliefs that would be advantageous for us to know at this time?

13. List the last three ministries you have held and how long at each church.

    a. _____ Dates: _____

    b. _____ Dates: _____

    c. _____ Dates: _____

14. How much time are you required to give to notify the church where you now serve, should you desire to make a change? _____

15. List eight references we might contact (one businessman, one neighbor, an elder where you serve, one college professor and four others of your choosing):

a. _____

b. _____

c. _____

d. _____

e. _____

f. _____

g. _____

h. _____

16. Please give an outline as to how you organize your average day as minister/evangelist:

17. Please list in order of importance (as you see it) the following as they relate to your ministry; Teaching, Preaching, Pastoral work, Leadership training, Counseling, Visitation/evangelism, Youth, Music, Other . . . .

1.   6.

2.   7.

3.   8.

4.   9.

5.

18. Additional information you desire to supply will be deeply appreciated.

VII
FORMAL ORGANIZATION OF THE NEW CHURCH

It is customary to have a "Charter Signing" or "Charter Opening" on the first Sunday that formal worship services are held. At this time those who desire to be a member of the new church come to the front of the meeting place at the close of the morning worship service and sign the new charter. A suggested form for a charter is on page 38.

The charter is placed in attractive booklet form with additional pages for the enrollees. There should be a space for each person to sign. It would be well for the charter or a copy to be available at the "planning sessions" for discussion and explanations.

After a person has signed the charter, the church clerk notifies the church from which they are transferring. On page 39 will be a form that can be used for this purpose.

The charter can be left open for signatures at each public service for a short period of time. Some churches limit the time to as little as one month. Others may decide to hold the charter open for as long as six months or even a year.

The charter can be a simple affair as the form enclosed, or it can be elaborate. One church had their's printed on embossed paper, see page 39, each member signed it, then it was photographed and copies suitable for framing were given to the signers.

Legal incorporation is a necessity in my opinion. It will protect each member from the possibility of individual law suits. It makes the entire congregation a legal entity. To the best of my knowledge legal incorporation is necessary if the congregation is to purchase and hold title to real estate or intends to secure a loan from a recognized lending agency.

Lawyer Luther Burris speaks about the advisability to incorporate in an article "Advisable to Incorporate."

The writer prefers, then, to consider the advisability of a church incorporating, with the attendant responsibility of establishing articles of incorporation. While no state or federal laws require a local congregation derivative of the Restoration movement to be incorporated in the legal sense, it is nonetheless desirable that each congregation do so, for several reasons, the principal ones being:

Firstly, it is a unique mark of religious freedom for any local congregation to have the legal right to incorporate! The overwhelming majority of the churches in Christendom today, being denominationally affiliated, are under some measure of control by a higher, ecclesiastical authority and thus do not have unqualified title to or control of their church property. Hence, such denominationally controlled churches could not locally incorporate, even if they wished to do so!

Secondly, incorporation indicates to the world at large that the legal and civil affairs of the particular congregation involved are being conducted on a business-like basis.

Thirdly, a golden opportunity is afforded to recite, in an official, recorded instrument (which is usually recorded in the offices of the secretary of state and the county court clerk), the basic position of the New Testament churches in this movement. Typically, the purpose of the incorporated congregation is to establish (or maintain, as the case may be) a church which is known among religious bodies as an undenominational Christian church or Church of Christ, whose members are known as Christians only, whose form of church government is strictly and absolutely congregational, whose sole rule of faith and practice is the New Testament itself, and in which congregation the two ordinances of the New Testament church (Baptism and the Lord's Supper) are observed in the manner of the primitive church; namely, the former by immersion only, and the latter each Lord's day (Sunday). When such a brief recitation of the basic principles of the Restoration movement is accompanied by a "latter-day declaration of independence" from any form of ecclesiastical control or affiliation, and a clear proscription against an absorption of the incorporated congregation into any type of denomination by merger . . . the writer submits that the Scriptural independence of the incorporated congregation will have been unequivocally enunciated before the state and the world at large. . . .

The incorporation should follow the procedure of being "not-for-profit."

Each state varies as to its requirements for incorporation "not-for-profit." It is best to write the respective secretary of state in the location of the desired incorporation. Be sure and state your desire for forms for a "not-for-profit" corporation.

The state of Illinois recognizes county incorporation. It is less expensive and easier to obtain and is as valid as a state approved corporation. A form used in Illinois and instructions for preparing it are to be found on pages 40-41. After a form is completed it is to be recorded at the County Recorder. Other states may do the same.

The Scriptures do not speak as to how a congregation conducts its business, such as elections of elders and deacons, holding congregational meetings, elections of treasurer, Bible School superintendents, church clerk, special meetings, etc. Of course the qualifications for elders and deacons are found in the New Testament (Acts 6:1-6; I Timothy 3:1-13; Titus 1:5-9; I Peter 5:1-5). Paul says in I Corinthians 14:40, "Let all things be done properly and in an orderly manner." A congregation will naturally develop an unwritten set of rules or the minutes of the elders and deacons meetings will govern business procedures.

By-laws, prepared in a simple matter, can be of great value in determining congregational procedures and to fulfill Paul's admonition to us in I

Corinthians 14:40.   By-laws can be cumbersome and a handicap or they can be guidelines for an efficient and effective service by the congregation and the elders and deacons.   By-laws are worth as much as the congregation that develops them. They do not guarantee a faithful and Scriptural church. If liberalism becomes the way of life of the church, the congregation can amend their by-laws to suit their lack of spirituality; their desire not to be guided by God's Word. For a sample Constitution and by-laws see pages 42-46.

It is wise for each congregation to gain Internal Revenue Service exemption for their individual congregation. This could forestall any future problems that could arise over income exemption. Forms for this can be secured from the local Internal Revenue Service Office or the Post Office.

When a congregation purchases property, or erects a house of worship, they can apply at the county courthouse for property tax exemption. Procedure will vary for this from state to state.

If a congregation desires to achieve recognition as being exempt from paying sales taxes, inquiries should be made from the Secretary of State's office. Again each state has its own laws governing this matter. Many states issue "numbers" or forms to use when a church purchases items that bear sales taxes.

_____, _____
               City   State

We, the undersigned, hereby enroll our names as charter members of the
_____ Christian Church and declare our purpose to be as
follows:

(1) To form an organization of obedient believers in Jesus of Nazareth as
the Christ, the Son of the Living God, the resurrected Christ.

(2) That this organization shall use the Bible, God's Word, as its one and only
rule of faith and practice.

(3) That the terms of admission to this organization shall be identical with the
gospel terms of pardon of sin as set forth in the New Testament. The act of
faith and repentance brings forth a confession of faith in Christ and the
believer is baptized into Christ for the forgiveness of his sins.

(4) That the purpose of the congregation shall be to carry out the commands
of Christ as suggested in the Great Commission;   to preach the simple
and entire gospel of divine pardon, Christian life and Christian duty, at home
and abroad; to encourage and admonish each other to mutual edification
and Christ-likeness; and to lend our individual and organized aid and support for the relief of distressed humanity and to all moral and civic better-
ment.

(5) To love one another as God so loves us without discrimination as to race
and color.

In witness, whereof we have affixed our signatures:

Dear Brethren in Christ:

Greetings in the name of Christ our Lord and Saviour.

In order that you may keep your records in order we are hereby notifying you that

_____

_____

_____

_____

became a member(s) of our congregation.

May God continue to bless you as His will is being done in your congregation.

In Christian Love,

_____

CHARTER MEMBERSHIP
of the

city   state   zip

WE, THE UNDERSIGNED, HEREBY DECLARE OUR INTENTIONS TO ORGANIZE A NEW CONGREGATION OF OBEDIENT BELIEVERS IN JESUS CHRIST, THE ONLY BEGOTTEN SON OF THE LIVING GOD. WE WILL USE THE BIBLE, GOD'S WORD, AS OUR ONLY RULE OF FAITH AND PRACTICE. PERSONS WILL BE RECEIVED INTO ACTIVE MEMBERSHIP, WITHOUT DISCRIMINATION, WHO REPENT FROM SIN, CONFESS FAITH IN CHRIST, AND ARE BAPTIZED INTO HIM. IN FORMING THIS CONGREGATION, WE PROPOSE TO FURTHER THE KINGDOM OF OUR LORD BY PRESENTING THE GOSPEL OF DIVINE LOVE AND PARDON. WE WILL ENCOURAGE ONE ANOTHER TO FAITHFUL GROWTH IN CHRISTLIKENESS AND HELP LIFT FALLEN MEN EVERYWHERE TO HIS GLORY.

AFFIDAVIT OF INCORPORATION OR ORGANIZATION

STATE OF ILLINOIS)
COUNTY OF _____)

I, _____ do solemnly swear, that at

a meeting of the members of the _____

_____, held at _____ , in the

county of _____ , and state of Illinois, on

the _____ day of _____, A.D. 19___, for

that purpose, following persons were elected trustees:

1. _____

2. _____

3. _____

according to the rules and usages of such church. And said church adopted

as its corporate name _____

And at this meeting this affiant acted as secretary.

_____
(name of affiant)

Place notarial seal here

Subscribed and sworn to before me this _____ day of _____, A.D.
19___.

INSTRUCTION SHEET FOR
"AFFIDAVIT OF INCORPORATION OR ORGANIZATION"

Instruction sheet for completing the "affidavit of organization or incorporation"; the chairman or secretary of such meeting shall, as soon as possible after the meeting, make and file in the office of the recorder of deeds in the county in which such congregation, church or society is organized (which shall be recorded by such recorder) an affidavit, substantially in the following form:

(see page 40)

AMENDMENTS: Such congregation, church or society may change its name or make other amendment to its original affidavit of incorporation by passing a resolution of such amendment in accordance with the rules and usages of such congregation, church or society and filing an affidavit to that effect in the office of the recorder of deeds, in the county in which such congregation, church or society is located.

EVIDENCE: Such affidavit, or a copy thereof duly certified by the recorder, shall be received as evidence of the due incorporation of such congregation, church or society.

CONSTITUTION AND BY-LAWS

Article I — Name.

This organization is incorporated under the laws of _____ as the

_____ Church.

(name)

Article II — Purpose.

The purpose of this church is to:

a. Worship God through Jesus Christ His Son.
b. Preach and teach the Gospel of Jesus Christ.
c. Support missionary and benevolent undertakings that are true to the Word of God.
d. Do good to all men.
e. Seek the restoration of the church as Jesus established it.
f. Seek out all men, regardless of race, color or creed, and teach them of Jesus Christ and His Word, hoping to win them for Christ.

Article III — Government.

Section 1. Autonomy . . .

a. It is specifically understood that this church is strictly autonomous and congregational in its government. It is subject to no other ecclesiastical body whatever.
b. It is to be understood that this church is at liberty to co-operate as it desires with other congregations.

Section 2. Leadership . . .

a. Leadership Committee: Composed of men (members) who are selected by the congregation. They will serve until such a time that they are removed or elders and deacons are slected by the congregation. The minister will also serve with the Leadership Committee or board as a non-voting member.
b. The organizing evangelist or an elder from a sister congregation may be invited to serve on the Leadership Committee as a non-voting member or members. The invitation is to come from the Church Board or Leadership Committee to serve.

Section 3. Official Church Board . . .

a. The official Church Board shall be comprised of the elders, deacons, and the minister (non-voting member). They shall care for the routine business of the church. They shall bring before the congregation for its approval any unusual business such as:

   (1) Capital outlay (building, grounds, etc.)
   (2) Extending a call to a minister.
   (3) Election of elders, deacons, church clerk, financial secretary, treasurer, Bible School superintendent, and the trustees.
   (4) The annual budget.

42

b. At the first meeting after the annual election of elders or deacons or a Leadership Committee they will elect a chairman, secretary and other officers as desired or needed. When the official board is composed of elders and deacons, the chairman shall be an elder.

c. For other non-voting members of the board or Leadership Committee, see Article III, Section 2.

Section 4. The Eldership . . .

a. Responsibility for the spiritual matters and welfare of the church is vested in the congregation's elders, who are elected by it. The number of elders shall be established by the official Church Board according to the need and the availability of Scripturally qualified men.

b. This church takes the Bible as its only rule of faith and practice, and Christ is its only creed. The decisions taken and the policies laid down by the elders on spiritual matters are always to be in accordance with the Bible's teaching for the church.

Section 5. Deacons . . .

a. The number of deacons shall be determined by the Church Board and the availability of Scripturally qualified men. The deacons shall co-operate with the elders in promoting the spiritual growth and welfare of the church.

Article IV — Membership.

Section 1. How to become a member . . .

a. Any person professing faith in the Lord Jesus Christ and showing evidence of repentance by public confession of Jesus Christ as the Son of God, upon being baptized may become a member of this congregation.

b. Members of other congregations may be received into this congregation provided they have obeyed their Lord in faith, repentance, confession of faith, and have been baptized into Christ.

Section 2. Termination of Membership . . .

Membership is voluntary and may be terminated at the member's request.

Section 3. Duties of Members . . .

Members of this church are to be faithful in all Christian duties; to attend regularly the services of the church, and especially to be faithful in attendance at the worship services; to give regularly of money and time to the support of the church and its activities; and, in general, to "walk worthily" of their calling as children of God.

Section 4. Active Members . . .

The active members of this church shall be those members who are regular in attendance and participation in the work of the church as stated in Section 3. Only the active members (16 years old and older) have the right to vote and to hold office. (See Article VI, Section 4.)

Article V — Officers.

Section 1. Selection of officers . . .

a. A nominating committee shall be selected by the chairman of the Church Board, subject to the approval of the board. This committee shall be composed of at least two elders, one deacon and one member of the congregation. The committee shall solicit nominations from the congregation (urging the selection of Scripturally qualified men), check on the nominee's Scriptural qualifications and willingness to serve, and draw up for each office a list of nominated persons found qualified and willing to serve. The resulting list shall be posted at least two weeks before the Annual Election. At the Annual Election the church will elect officers from this list (by ballot).

b. All officers of this church . . . elders, deacons, church clerk, financial secretary, treasurer, Bible school superintendent, and trustees . . . shall be elected by the majority vote of the congregation in accordance with Article VI, and should be 21 years of age or older. The term of office for elders, deacons, and trustees shall be for one, two, and three years respectively to permit election of officers each year.   The balance of officers shall be elected for one year.

c. After serving two consecutive terms of service, an elder, deacon, or trustee shall not serve for a period of one year.

Section 2. The Selection of a minister . . .

a. The elders (or Leadership Committee) shall constitute the Pulpit Committee when a minister is to be called, and shall recommend one candidate at a time for the pulpit to the official board and the congregation for approval.

b. Said minister shall not be engaged, however, except by a two-thirds majority vote of the congregation, in accordance with Article VI.

c. The minister shall be called for an indefinite period. Either the minister or the elders, or the Leadership Committee, upon approval of the congregation, may terminate the minister's service upon a 60-day notice by either party.

d. A contract shall be negotiated with the prospective minister by the elders or Leadership Committee and with final approval by the congregation.

Article VI — Meetings and Elections.

Section 1. Meetings to be held . . .

Robert's Rules of Order shall regulate the proceedings of all meetings.

a. The annual business meeting of the congregation shall be held in February. The Church Board or Leadership Committee shall select from its members a congregational chairman and he shall preside at congregational meetings. The purpose of this meeting shall be to transact business of the congregation and to receive the annual reports of various officers and offices, such as: elders and deacons, treasurer, financial secretary, church clerk, Bible School superintendent, and

44

various committees as designated by the Church Board. The minister shall also submit a written report to the congregation. Written reports should also be submitted by classes and Men's and Ladies' Groups.

b. A meeting of the congregation for the purpose of electing the officers of the church as listed in Article V shall be held annually in November. At this time the annual budget shall also be voted upon by the congregation.

c. At least once a month the Church Board (Leadership Committee) shall meet to conduct the business of the church on a previously designated date. The members present at a duly called meeting shall constitute a quorum. New officers of the church, elected in November, shall take office on the first of the year. The church shall operate on the calendar year basis.

d. At a specifically called meeting of the Church Board or Leadership Committee, two-thirds of board members shall constitute a quorum.

Section 2. Special Meetings of the Congregation . . .

Special meetings of the congregation shall be announced at least one Lord's Day prior to the date of the proposed meeting. However, the official Church Board or Leadership Committee may waive this provision, provided written notice is sent by mail to the last known address of each active member of the congregation in time for said notice to have been delivered at least twenty-four hours before the time of said meeting.

Section 3. Quorum for Meetings of Congregation . . .

A quorum for meetings of the congregation shall consist of one-third or more of the active members. (See Article IV, Section 4.)

Section 4. Eligibility to Vote . . .

Only those members of the congregation who are active and who are sixteen years of age or over shall vote.

Article VII — Constitution and By-Laws.

This Constitution and By-Laws may be amended by a two-thirds majority vote at any business meeting of the congregation, in accordance with Article VI. All proposed amendments shall be posted in a conspicuous place in the church building or meeting place, and shall have the attention of the congregation verbally called to them during the services of at least two successive Lord's Days before the time of the meeting at which they are to be voted upon.

Article VIII — Property.

Section 1. Trustees . . .

The trustees shall be selected in accordance with Article V. They shall have no power to buy, sell, lease or mortgage any property of the congregation without a majority vote of the members in a duly called congregational meeting (see Article VI). The trustees shall be selected from among the elders and deacons or the Leadership Committee and shall only hold in trust the property of the congregation.

Section 2. Dissolution Provisions . . .

Upon the dissolution of the corporation, the Board of Trustees shall, afteking provision for the payment of all liabilities of the corporation, dispose of all of the assets of the corporation exclusively for the purpose of the corporation in such manner, or to such organizations organized and operated exclusively for charitable, educational, religious or scientific purposes as shall at the time qualify as an exempt organization or organizations under Section 501 (c) (3) of the Internal Revenue Code of 1954 (or to corresponding provision of any future United States Internal Revenue Law). as the Trustees shall determine. Any such assets not so disposed of shall be disposed by the Court of Common Pleas of the county in which the principal office of the corporation is then located, exclusively for which purpose or to such organizations or organization as said court shall determine, which are organized and operating exclusively for such purposes.

No part of the net earnings of the corporation shall inure to the benefit of, or be distributable to, its members, trustees, officers, or other private persons except that the corporation shall be authorized and empowered to pay reasonable compensation for services rendered and to make payments and distributions to furtherance of the purposes set forth elsewhere. No substantial part of the activities of the corporation shall be carrying on of propaganda, or otherwise attempting to influence legislation, and the corporation shall not participate in, or intervene in (including the publishing or distribution of statements) any political campaign on behalf of any candidate for public office. Notwithstanding any other provision of these articles, the corporation shall not carry on any activities not permitted to be carried on (a) by a corporation exempt from Federal Income Tax under Section 501 (c) (3) of the Internal Revenue Code of 1954 (or the corresponding provision of any future United States Internal Revenue Law) or (b) by a corporation, contributions to which are deductible under section 170 (c) (2) of the Internal Revenue Law).

Section 3. Final Dissolution . . .

In the event that this congregation (organization should be permanently dissolved the remaining assets are to be permanently dedicated to

---

This is a non-profit religious organization with the Federal Exemption number of _____.

This Constitution and By-Laws of the _____

(name)

became effective on _____, 19____

(date)

Signed _____

Signed _____

Signed _____

VIII

THE BIBLE SCHOOL IN THE NEW CHURCH

 The Bible School or Sunday School is a very important part of the new congregation. It is one of the links to be forged for appealing to the unchurched and the unsaved. Children can be reached and parents influenced for Christ by a well-planned Bible School. Perhaps the following poem, author unknown, expresses well the importance of Bible School and the role a dedicated teacher has:

I took a piece of plastic clay
And idly fashioned it one day
And, as my fingers pressed it still,
It moved and yielded to my will.

I came again when days were past,
The bit of clay was hard at last.
The form I gave it, it still bore,
But I could change that form no more.

I took a piece of living clay,
And gently formed it day by day
And molded with my power and art
A young child's soft and yielding heart.

I came again when years were gone
It was a man I looked upon:
He still that early impress wore,
And I could change him never more.

Often in a new church with a small nucleus, there may not be enough qualified teachers, and students may also be scarce. It may not be possible to have all the desired classes at the beginning.

Take a poll of the prospective members and their children. Arrive at a conclusion as to how many students and teachers will be available. Perhaps it

47

will be necessary to combine various ages or groupings such as: Nursery, age one; Preschool, ages two, three and four; ages five and six; ages seven, eight and nine; ages ten, eleven and twelve; the Teens; and adults. Or perhaps some other grouping would be more appropriate for your new church. See pages 51-52 for a form that may be of value to you in arranging your classes and in assigning your teachers.

As to Bible School supplies and literature, the Standard Publishing, 8121 Hamilton Avenue, Cincinnati, Ohio 45231, is a splendid source of true-to-the-Bible literature. Of course there are many, many other publishing companies who publish and sell Bible School literature. Each company should be checked on whether or not they are true-to-the Bible. Each teacher, initially, can assume the responsibility for her own crayons, scissors, pencils, paste, etc. Later as the funds are more plentiful the church can purchase these necessary supplies.

If the church begins in the middle of a quarter, perhaps the teachers can arrange to use supplies that are procured from the "Mother Church" or a neighboring sister church.

In the selection of a Bible School co-ordinator (superintendent) the utmost care must be exercised. The late James DeForest Murch, the noted educator, has set forth qualifications that are worthy of note. He said of the Bible School superintendent, (1) "Must be a Christian and member of the local congregation; (2) Must be an executive with vision; (3) Should be an educator and student; (4) Should be diplomatic and humble; (5) Should be efficient and untiring; (6) Willing to acquire knowledge of the work to be done and then do it."

The duties of the co-ordinator of the Bible School will be to direct the course of the whole school. Of course, the general outlines will be defined by the congregation or Leadership Committee or the Board of Elders. The superintendent must know what is being done and planned by the teachers and the departments. This Bible School leader should be visionary in suggesting plans and should work to carry them out. Much of the growth of the new church's Bible School and the whole church will depend upon the Bible School superintendent or co-ordinator.

Meticulous must be the "key word" in keeping records of class attendance, offerings, visitors, etc. Well-kept records by an efficient secretary of a Bible School class or of the whole Bible School will be of inestimable value to a new church. Here are some reasons for efficient record keeping:

a. Provides information concerning pupils of all ages. Records are more than an effort to count heads and pennies. They tell a story that will not be forgotten.
b. Records teach pupils character-building habits—faithfulness, reverence, and responsibility.
c. Records provide information regarding eligibility for awards, recognition, and promotion.
d. They aid the school in doing a better job of teaching. Records provide a check on the efficiency of the teacher and the pupil.

e. Well-kept records and the use of those records will guarantee that the school can hold the gains made in new contacts.

f. Records will provide the needed information concerning absentees and prospects.

g. They will assist in the evangelistic program of the church by furnishing names of individuals and family prospects. Records of church membership or lack of church membership can be vital to the success or failure of the church's evangelistic effort. They will also assist in conservation of the new members with doctrinal and social follow-up.

h. Records will give an up-to-date statistical picture of the total school by departments, by classes, and by students. From this picture the leadership of a new church can determine the needs, aims, and goals for the future. They can plan to grow!

i. If the keeping of records begins in the infancy of a new Bible School and church, they will probably be kept diligently from then on.

A new Bible School may wish to break with tradition and to dispense with the "opening exercise." There are many reasons for doing so, but the greatest is the opportunity for more time for teaching the Bible. The teachers do not feel pressed for time, so they can do justice to teaching the vital lesson. If the decision of the congregation is to continue the "opening exercise" then provision should be made in the planning sessions for structuring the "opening exercise." Ten to fifteen minutes should be long enough and it must be peppy as well as inspiring. Usually an hour is the length of time allotted to Bible School. Secure a bell for use in warning of the time and the dismissal of classes.

As to classroom space for the Bible School of a new church, this can be a real problem, especially if the church is rented space from a public school or a lodge hall is being used. The use of public school classrooms can often lead to problems. School teachers often resent the intrusion of Bible School students or their rooms being used during "off hours." Materials, blackboards, displays, desks, etc. can be and are often disturbed by curious Bible School students and even by Bible School teachers. Complaints are made to the principals! Churches have been known to have been denied the use of public school buildings because of this very problem.

When arrangements are made to rent or use a public school building or any building for that matter, consideration must be given to obtaining classroom space. If an all-purpose room or a gym is being used, be sure and secure permission to use the adjacent hallways and stage area. Another factor not to be overlooked is permission to use the restrooms. By the wise use of the gym or all-purpose room and the hallways and the stage area, adequate classroom space has usually been found. It may be inconvenient, but then we must not forget our goal, "estalbishing this church for the glory of Christ and to win souls to Christ." Interesting true-to-the-Bible lessons by a dedicated teacher can overcome most obstacles.

Storage space, with a lock, is almost a must, for the Bible School and the infant church. It will be used for Bible School materials, hymnbooks, communion ware, etc. Carrying these necessary items back and forth from homes can be a real chore. The committee on renting the building should keep this storage space in mind when arranging for the lease.

Perhaps a word should be said about "cleaning-up" after Bible school and worship services. Usually this will be in the agreement signed with the school authorities. Housekeeping chores may be unpleasant and time consuming but very necessary to the thoughtful Christian.

A WORK SHEET FOR SELECTING BIBLE SCHOOL TEACHERS AND THEIR ASSISTANTS

Cradle Roll ministry (age 0 to one year) _____

    Assistant teacher _____

Nursery, Age 1 _____

    Assistant teacher _____

Nursery, Age 2 _____

    Assistant teacher _____

Nursery, Age 3 _____

    Assistant teacher

Preschool, Age 4 _____

    Assistant teacher

Preschool, Age 5 _____

    Assistant teacher

Primary, Grade one _____

    Assistant teacher _____

Primary, Grade two _____

    Assistant teacher _____

Junior, Grade three _____

    Assistant teacher _____

Junior, Grade four _____

    Assistant teacher _____

Middler, Grade five _____

    Assistant teacher _____

Middler, Grade six _____

    Assistant teacher _____

Junior Hi, Grade seven _____

    Assistant teacher _____

Junior Hi, Grade eight _____

    Assistant teacher _____

Niners, Grade nine _____

    Team teacher _____

Senior Hi, Grades ten, eleven and twelve _____

    Team teacher _____

College (out of high school and not married) _____

    Team teacher _____

Adult class _____

    Team teacher _____

Note: A combination of classes may be necessary for a small congregation.

IX
PROVIDING EQUIPMENT FOR THE NEW CHURCH

Always, whenever a new church is being considered, the question of the necessary equipment arises. The amount of needed equipment of course varies with the size of the nucleus and the meeting place available.

An organ or piano will probably be needed. Often this will be available at the school, hall, etc. that is being rented. Inquiry should be made when renting arrangements are made. Otherwise, the new church may secure their own instrument. Again, arrangements must be made with the landlord, school principal, etc.

Many schools and halls have portable speaking rostrums. If not, one may be borrowed from a local church, or constructed by a friendly craftsman. It would be convenient if it was large enough for storing hymnals and communion ware and was on castors, after use it could be stored near the space used for worship.

Hymnals are often secured from a neighboring church. These may be used, or new, it depends on how fortunate the new congregation is. An ad in a religious journal would possibly bring a large number of offers of used songbooks.

Recommendation is made that the new church begin by using bulletins. The bulletin covers can be turned out by a church with an offset press or they can be purchased. The exterior of the bulletin (pages one and four) can be printed and the interior can be mimeographed from Sunday to Sunday. These bulletin covers can also be used for mailing purposes or in visitation. Suggested samples are included on pages 60-65.

Communion ware and offering plates often are secured from a neighboring brotherhood church or the "Mother Church." Many times when an established congregation buys new communion ware, the used ware is stored away, yet it is useable and presentable. One of the first items of equipment to be purchased should be new and attractive communion ware and offering plates. It must not be forgotten that appearance is important and this is the Lord's Supper! Communion cloths must be kept clean, neat and snowy white.

A guest book or register is very worthwhile and most visitors appreciate being asked to register. This can be invaluable for future reference and to obtain the names and addresses of visitors that may not fill out an "attendance card."

Chairs and tables are almost always available in rented facilities. Arrangements should be made to use these when rental procedures are made. There should also be an understanding as to who will set-up the chairs and tables and who will take them down. Some schools, lodges, etc. insist upon these chores being done by their custodian and he will be compensated by the renter. If chairs and tables are not available in the rented building, then they may be borrowed from a neighboring church or lodge, etc. It may be necessary to purchase them or to build tables that will fold. Occasionally, a man that is handy with tools will construct benches for the children and tables to match. These will be sized for various ages, etc.

Such things as flags, backdrops, crosses, etc. all aid and create a worshipful atmosphere. These are needed to overcome bareness and drabness of a multi-purpose room or gym. To overcome the reluctance of some people to worship in a "school gym" it will be necessary for the leaders of the new church to use their imagination and talents to plan and to develop that which will assist in leading the worshiper closer to his Lord.

Much has been said in the chapter on "The Bible School" about the necessity of keeping adequate records. The same applies to the church as a whole. Basic record supplies are essential to the keeping of permanent and proper records. If, from the beginning, good records are kept, it will be a blessing to the church and will aid tremendously in its growth. An excellent source for records and supplies will be your publishing house or Basic Church-Record Supplies. (See page 77 for additional information.)

Portable nursery supplies are often very vital to the health and development of an infant church. Young, unchurched mothers and fathers, being reached for Christ, are not reachable when being distracted by their infants. A well attended nursery supplied with adequate furniture and staffed by loving and dedicated ladies can often be a great blessing to a new church. It will attract young couples with children. Nursery equipment can often be borrowed or bought used. Sometimes storage can be a major problem. Hopefully, arrangements can be made at the public school, etc. for storage. If not, many times concerned leaders have used their cars, station wagons, trucks to transport nursery equipment each Sunday. Should any reminder be given to the necessity of cleanliness of the equipment, sheets, pillows, pads, etc.?

Right from the beginning, the need for office equipment will be evident. Perhaps some of the first funds available to a new congregation could be wisely spent to buy office equipment and supplies. A good rebuilt or new mimeograph, if possible, will prove invaluable to a new congregation. Along with this will be needed a typewriter, new, if at all possible. It should be a heavy duty office typewriter that will stand up under the typing of stencils and being used by inexperienced typists. When the first budget is prepared, provision must be made for office equipment and supplies. Often when a church procrastinates in obtaining office equipment and supplies in its infancy, it will be even more difficult to set aside funds for office equipment when a church becomes involved in purchasing a building site and building a house of worship.

A check list for suggested needed equipment to make a new church operational is to be found on page 56.

A LIST OF EQUIPMENT NEEDED FOR A NEW CHURCH

1. Piano and/or organ
2. Pulpit
3. Hymnals
4. Bulletins
5. Communion ware—communion cloths
6. Guest book
7. Chairs
8. Tables
9. Offering trays
10. Flags
11. A back drop
12. Signs
13. Offering envelopes.
14. Basic record keeping supplies:
    a. Secretary book.
    b. Visitation cards.
    c. Membership book.
    d. Treasurer's book.
    e. Financial secretary's book.
    f. Historian's book or file.
    g. Church clerk's materials.

15. Cribs and Nursery supplies
16. Office supplies:
    a. Mimeograph or offset press.
    b. Typewriter
    c. Paper, ink, etc.
    d. Stencils, etc.

17. Other needs:

X

PUBLICIZING THE NEW CHURCH

 One of the most important positions in a new church is that of the "publicity chairman." She or he can render a service to the Lord that can have far-reaching benefits and rewards for the church. With the use of a pen and paper and a camera with black and white film, a dedicated and inquisitive Christian as publicity chairman can do much to witness for Christ and the new congregation.

The right material, interesting and concise, submitted for publication or for radio, will be invaluable to the planting of a new church. Here are some brief tips on publicity. These pointers are probably familiar to every writer but are worth repeating and applying to the needs of church publicity and the preparing of copy.

In preparing material to be released for publication, the writer should always keep in mind five categories. These are known in writers' circles as the five W's and traditionally the five W's form the basic elements of a news release. The five W's are Who, What, When, Where, and Why. WHO is involved? WHAT happened? WHEN did it happen? WHERE did it happen? WHY did it happen? The five W's are usually grouped into the first few sentences or the first two or three paragraphs of the news release. This is true whether or not the story is for the newspaper, church newsletter or the radio or perhaps for television. Together the five W's become the points of emphasis of your story. The reader can tell at a glance the important points of the story concerning your church and should remember them for future reference. He then has the facts which are necessary. He may continue to read for further details.

The news release has been prepared, now where do you take it or send it for publication? Or perhaps you can even release it on the telephone, depending upon the church editor of the local newspaper. The sources available to the publicity chairman of a new church are numerous.

The national church publications are always ready to print **news** about new churches beginning and their progress. They often have special sections or columns set aside for progress reports of new churches. Many brotherhood religious magazines will also publish good black and white glossy pictures of your newsworthy activities.

Many Christian colleges, especially if the new church is in their general geographical area or if one of their alumni is associated with the new church, will gladly publicize the new church's activities and progress in their newsletters.

Local churches of the same faith and sometimes otherwise will often give space in their newsletters and Sunday bulletins. News releases should be sent to them as a matter of courtesy.

In most urban communities there will be found "Shopper" news sheets. These are distributed to almost every home in a given area free of charge. Many of these papers will take most all of the news items you can give them. They will also print church ads, usually very reasonbly. The householders **do** scan this type of paper.

The knowledgeable publicity chairman will not forget the old standbys in sources of publicity such as the local daily or weekly newspapers, radio and television. These will always use good newsy items and pictures. A visit to the local newspaper, radio and television station to meet the church editor can be very beneficial. Also, not to be forgotten, is an occasional thank you note and even small gifts of appreciation.

Of special interest and of great value to the publicity minded congregation will be brochures which will feature the new church and its activities. These can be produced rather inexpensively through the use of the offset press and mimeograph. Such brochures can be distributed from house to house when canvassing and can be used by the members and the minister in visitation. In fact, I dislike to make a call unless I have some identifying material in hand to give or to leave. If the prospect is not home a brochure can be left in the door. The call will not be entirely wasted. Several copies of these inexpensive brochures are included on pages 60-65.

These brochure fronts are also often used for the Sunday bulletins. When they are being prepared (printed) the interior is left blank for Sunday to Sunday use.

Letter writing, telephoning friends and members, posters for businesses and public buildings are also other forms of publicity that can often be used to very good advantage depending upon the circumstances.

Just prior to the formal beginning of worship services and Bible School of the new church, "door-to-door" advertising must be done. A special poster, folder, handbill or brochure can be prepared for this occasion. See page 59 for a sample copy. Many times neighboring churches or college students will assist in this much needed promotion.

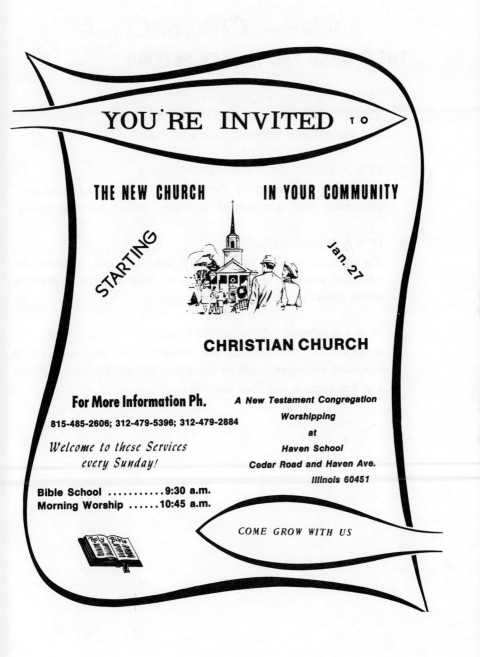

Suburban Christian Church

THE CHURCH YOU'VE BEEN SEEKING

1. IT'S A FRIENDLY CHURCH !
You'll enjoy the hearty welcome, the friendly atmosphere, and the sincere interest shown in YOU !

2. IT'S A BIBLE-BELIEVING CHURCH !
We proclaim the whole Gospel of Christ, and provide a preaching and a pastoral ministry suited to your needs.

3. IT'S A BUSY CHURCH !
We have an active and growing Bible School, a warm devotional worship service! Our activities and plans make a place for every person of every age.

4. IT'S A GROWING CONGREGATION !
Evangelistic in doctrine and practice, we are enjoying a constant increase, both in our Bible School (Sunday School) and our regular worship services.

Suburban

Christian Church

SUBURBAN CHRISTIAN CHURCH
Located at: 7535 Taft Street
Phone: 219-769-8675

ATTEND CHURCH SUNDAY

"The Church That Cares About You"

A WORD OF INTRODUCTION

We are a non-denominational New Testament congregation, part of a world-wide movement to restore the essentials of apostolic Christianity as a means to the unity of all Christian believers. We are a free, democratic, friendly people. We believe in Biblical Christianity and endeavor to lead lives of faithfulness and devotion. We acknowledge Jesus Christ as the divine Son of God, and Lord and Savior. We accept the Bible as the inspired record of God's revelation to man. We believe that the New Testament is the only divine rule of faith and practice given to the followers of Christ.

OUR LOCATION

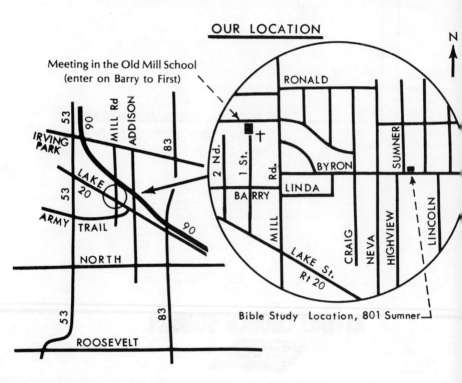

Meeting in the Old Mill School
(enter on Barry to First)

Bible Study Location, 801 Sumner

CHRISTIAN CHURCH

MEETING IN THE OLD MILL SCHOOL
848 NORTH MILL ROAD
ILLINOIS 60101

phone : 543-4632

Friendship and Fellowship

... IN CHRISTIAN LOVE

THE CHRISTIAN CHURCH

We believe and teach that Jesus Christ is the only begotten Son of God, and that he is the Savior of the world.

Our sole test of membership is belief in Christ and obedience to his teaching.

In accepting Christ, we believe that one's life should be lived in strict harmony with His teaching as revealed in the New Testament.

We have no creed but the Christ
We bear no name but his name
We study and preach no book but the Bible.

All Cases of Conversion Recorded in the New Testament
Are Found in The Book of Acts:

Philip   Acts 8:12 and 26:39
Paul and Ananias; Acts 9:17—18 and 22:12—16
Cornelius, Acts 10:44—48
Lydia, Acts 16:25—33
Crispus and the Corinthians, Acts 18:7—8
Disciples of John, Acts 19:1—5

We seek to follow the Biblical pattern in all things,   our conversion and our practices as a church. In keeping with the apostolic practice we have communion (the Lord's Supper) every first day of the week. (Acts 20:7). Our church government is a democracy in the truest form of the word. We choose Elders (Acts 14:23) and Deacons, (I Timothy 3:8—12) from among our eligible members, who serve the congregation. We seek and have full fellowship with all churches that acknowledge Christ as Lord and seek to obey Him in all things.

VISITORS: We invite you to have fellowship with us in the times of worship; let us together glorify our God! You are welcome to all the activities of the congregation. Above all do the will of Christ in your life.

A

warm
welcome
awaits
you

North Suburban

CHRISTIAN CHURCH

OUR PURPOSE: To preach and teach the Word of God
in love and to reach YOU for Christ.

XI

FINANCING THE NEW CHURCH

 Financing almost any program of the church is always a problem unless the congregation has been taught to give, because they ought to give, rather than to give out of necessity or pressure. Men are taught to tithe because of love of Christ rather than because of commandment. Earl C. Hargrove in his splendid booklet entitled "The Road to Satisfaction," points out "The only hope for the Christian is a gnawing spiritual dissatisfaction which is so strong it will lead him to pay the price for satisfaction." The Christian pays the price for satisfaction in the Lord by first giving of himself to the Lord and then by giving his time, talents, and material substance.

When Christians begin to give as the Lord has given to them (His all) then the church begins to overcome its financial problems.

Financial needs for a new congregation can be tremendous! Often this is a stumbling block to beginning a new church. Many Christians cannot visualize where the funds can be obtained to call a full-time evangelist, buy a building site, build a building, etc. There are many sources of funds.

First of all will be the sacrificial giving of the nucleus. They will need to tithe and more than tithe. They will walk in faith and not by sight in their planning for a new church. Stewardship of time, talent and money will be taught and promoted from the beginning. The habit of teaching stewardship must begin early in the life of a new church. **A good beginning for the infant church is to tithe its offerings for missions.** Budgets and goals should be considered and prepared. Offering envelopes should be used by all members, no matter how small the congregation. Correct records of giving and information concerning contributions should be made available to the congregation.

The following is a program of stewardship recommended for a new church or for any church for that matter.

1. Constant challenge and teaching on the need and blessing of giving.
2. Public reference by leaders and others as to what giving means to them. This can be done from the pulpit, church paper, at offering time, etc.
3. A challenging annual budget prepared in October.
4. Commitment time after congregational preparation (first week of December). Christians must give—why not planned giving? It is done to buy a car, home, etc.
5. Use large offering envelopes. Leaders are to set the example in giving. This includes the minister.

Secondly, as to the financial support for a minister, building site or new building, it would be a rarity for a new church to be self-sustaining from the very first. How many babies are able to sustain themselves? A "Mother Church" or sister congregation often is the best source of financial assistance as well as encouragement and moral support. Many well-established congregations have led out in planting new churches. They have gone so far as to furnish funds for a minister, to buy a building site and have assisted in erecting a house of worship. Some concerned, spiritually minded congregations have even mortgaged their own buildings to assist (Mother) a new church or have gone to the bank and co-signed a mortgage for a new church. Sister churches have also urged their members to purchase building bonds from the new church or have suggested loans to the new church.

Another source of funds for a new church is the self-supporting minister or his wife who may be employed. This of course limits the activities of the minister and his wife but has made it possible for many new churches to begin. The new church should understand and appreciate the sacrifice being made by the preacher and his wife and family. The leadership must assume many of the areas of service normally carried by the minister.

An Evangelistic Fellowship (Association) such as the Chicago District Evangelistic Association or the Central Illinois Evangelistic Association is another source of funds and moral support for a new church. These fellowships or associations combine the resources of many churches and individuals to make possible a new church or many new churches. Calvin Phillips set forth in "The Evangel" (October, 1968) very ably the advantages of a Fellowship or Association in planting new churches. He said in his article entitled, "Organizing to Meet the Challenge."

> . . . The task of adequately establishing churches to meet this ever growing and ever shifting population is enormous. How shall it be accomplished? One method is through an evangelistic association, such as the Chicago District Evangelistic Association. Other methods are helpful also, and are welcomed. Some of the characteristics of an evangelistic association that make it highly advantageous are:
>
> 1. **All churches can share.** No church is too small or too limited in resources to participate when resources are pooled through an association. We can do together what we cannot do separately.
>
> 2. **A cooperative group will tend to view the needs of an entire area** whereas one congregation is more likely to look only to adjacent communities. It is a fact of modern urban life that most people who live in a metropolitan area are unmindful of the needs and opportunities of communities other than their own.

3. Support will more likely be continuous. If contributions are made to one particular new work or to a minister who is beginning a particular new work, the support will probably be for a specified time and will then be terminated. But the need is just as great in another area. If funds are given through an association, they can be directed to a new field as soon as one is self supporting.

4. An association provides a channel through which gifts from churches outside an area may give and through which individuals may give. It makes for an orderly, responsible form of missionary endeavor. In most metropolitan areas churches in the Restoration Movement are neither large nor numerous. Help must come from other areas. An on-the-spot church planting association can become a vehicle for churches all over our land.

5. Ministers for new churches do not have to rely solely on their own efforts for support. More and more ministers are welcoming the challenge of leading in the establishment of a new congregation. It seems unfair to him to ask him to solicit. It is asking a great deal of a man to say, "We want you to establish a church here. Go and raise your support and come and do it." It is far better to say, "If you will come and establish a church, we will, with your help and God's grace, raise your support."

6. It is mutually stimulating and strengthening. Sharing together arouses interest among those who would otherwise not think of becoming personally involved. It gives confidence to those who fear to launch out. There are people in communities without one of our churches. These have led in the establishment of a church, to whom this possibility would never have occurred had they not seen others do it in their communities.

7. The financial load is more evenly distributed. Churches cost money. New churches cost a lot if money-membership is small. Often the families are young, land must be purchased, a building erected, supplies purchased, a minister's salary paid, and his home provided.

The burden can be great and the program retarded many years. Substantial assistance which an association can provide can lighten the burden and accelerate the work. A new congregation properly begun and adequately supported will, within ten years, return much more to the cause of the Kingdom than it received.

XII

SITE AND CONSTRUCTION FOR THE NEW CHURCH

One of the most important decisions a new church will make is the selection of a building site. I believe that the wrong decision as to location, size, type of community, terrain, zoning, restrictions, etc. of the site can affect adversely the development of the congregation. Professional advice should be sought when a site is to be purchased.

There are many things to be considered when evaluation of a proposed building site is being made. For the convenience of the site committee a site evaluation sheet is included on pages 72-73.

As to location, an area that is experiencing growth in single family homes or townhouses is excellent. It should be reasonably near a public school and located on a prominent street. Someone has well said, "Wherever the sign is located to guide you to the church building, that is where the building should have been."

The size of the site will depend upon the estimated future potential membership. Perhaps a good rule of thumb would be:

300 members and under ....at least 3 acres.
400 members ....at least 4 acres.
500 to 800 members ....at least 5 acres.
800 to 1500 members ....at least 10 acres.

Circumstance may dictate a variance to the above formula.

Off-street parking is a necessity and a requirement in most communities. Today many communities are requiring one parking space for each three persons being accommodated in the building at one time. Each space requires ten feet by thirty feet. County and city ordinances should be consulted as to legal requirements. Zoning regulations should also be checked as to off-street parking.

It is extremely important to consult an attorney as to title matters. In entering into an agreement to purchase, a clause should be in the contract stating that the site will be purchased if it can be used for church building purposes. Zoning laws and restrictions, set-backs, sanitary sewer requirements, easements, assessments (unpaid or future), etc. should be examined carefully before the contract is consummated.

It is also advisable to conduct test borings of the soil to see if it is suitable for buildings and foundations. A peat-bog or quick sand would be a poor basis for a building. If a septic system is to be used instead of city sewers then percolation tests should be made of the sub-soil. If drainage is poor or slow then problems will arise in the use or construction of a septic system. Again, professional assistance should be sought.

The orientation of a church building to the site is as important in many ways as the development of the floor plan or must be considered in the development of a master plan (future units). It is well to take into consideration the area of passenger unloading as well as the parking area, the sidewalks, landscaping, exposures in relationship to sun and wind, recreation areas, and adjoining parsonage, etc.

After the new church has purchased its site and is ready to consider its first building or unit the question often arises, "should they call an architect who 'specializes' in church buildings and church educational units or should they investigate a 'church-building' firm or corporation?" The building committee should do both! They should interview church architects and "church builders." They should be as astute in building for the Lord as they would be in buying or building a house for themselves. Surely they will spend much time in seeking the best for their situation and the funds available.

The architect selected must be a man who is able to visualize the House of God and its function. He should have experience in spiritual things and be able to relate them to wood, stone, brick, concrete and plastics.

If a "church builder" is selected, he or his architect must have the same qualifications as a privately employed architect. Also to be checked out are the credit qualifications of both of these. Examination of work done or buildings built should also be done.

The building committee or construction committee shall be responsible for oversight in all phases of the construction.

Some warnings are justified in regards to construction of buildings. Do not overbuild! It is better to provide room for expansion or to add another unit than to build beyond the capacity of the congregation to pay or to adequately use. In fact, it is always wise to consider and to provide in almost any building project the means to expand or to add on.

There are a few congregations that think "too small" in building. A careful analysis should be made of the congregation's ability to grow and to meet the payments on the new building. Perhaps professional advice should be sought in this matter.

Have all the necessary building permits been secured? Have your plans been submitted to the city planning commission or zoning committee for approval? Or perhaps the county equivalent? Have you obtained permission for the driveway from the city, county or state? How about sewer connections and water? Or septic system permit and tests?

As you are building, the need for changes in your plans (blueprints) may arise. Almost without exception, changes and improvements to the original plans, once the contracts have been let, will cost considerable additional money. Often it will cost at least twice as much as it would have cost if it had been in the original contract. So plan wisely and carefully that the Lord's money will be spent judiciously.

Insurance is a vital item for the church as well as for the contractors. Injuries, wind storms, fire, etc. can bring about terrific set-backs in time and finances. A building fund, gained sacrificially, can be lost overnight by an uninsured disaster. Adequate insurance to protect volunteer labor, church members and friends, as well as employees, and the building under construction is sensible, legally required in some states and morally right. Much embarrassment can be avoided by adequate and proper insurance.

Often when a new congregation is in a building program, the evangelistic effort suffers. This ought not to be. The church must continue to reach out for precious souls as it builds to house its program. A lapse in evangelism can be self-destructive to a congregation and to the program of the minister-evangelist. Perhaps this is why many ministers move to another church within a year after the building program is completed.

In financial matters, such as settling with the contractors, precautions must be taken to insure payment of all obligations. A "waiver of lien" by the contractors, suppliers of materials, lumber yards, etc. must be obtained before funds are disbursed. These forms "waiver of lien" can be obtained from an office supply firm or an attorney. Many churches have paid all their bills on time when building, only to find that the contractors had not paid for the lumber, brick, cement, plumbing supplies, even the labor. Consequently a "lien" is placed against their new building and it can be sold to satisfy the creditors.

SITE SELECTION WORK SHEET

Address_____ City_____

1. Location: ☐Downtown ☐Residential ☐Country Other _____

2. Size _____

3. Zoning: ☐Industrial ☐Commercial ☐Residential ☐Agricultural

    Other _____ Church building permit ☐yes ☐no
4. Restrictions: ☐One-story buildings only ☐Business only ☐No septic

    ☐Driveways Abstract covenants ☐yes ☐no

    Easements: Electric? ☐yes ☐no Gas? ☐yes ☐no
    Telephone? ☐yes ☐no
    Sewers? ☐yes ☐no Water? ☐yes ☐no
    Flood Plain? ☐yes ☐no

    Set back requirements? From the streets _____

    From the neighbors _____

5. Improvements: Paved streets? ☐yes ☐no
    Curbs and gutters? ☐yes ☐no
    Sidewalks? ☐yes ☐no City water? ☐yes ☐no
    Sewer lines? ☐yes ☐no   Electricity? ☐yes ☐no
    Natural gas? ☐yes ☐no Other_____

6. Title matters: Has an attorney been retained? ☐yes ☐no
    Is a good and merchantable title available? ☐yes ☐no

7. What are the future or unpaid assessments? _____

_____

8. Terrain: Well drained? ☐yes ☐no Sloping up? ☐yes ☐no
    Sloping down? ☐yes ☐no ☐Level ☐Hilly ☐Needs fill.
    ☐Swampy ☐Woody

9. Accessibility: Easy to enter by car? ☐yes ☐no Highway? ☐yes ☐no
    Within Walking distance of public transportation? ☐yes ☐no
    Public school nearby? ☐yes ☐no
    Adequate parking space available? ☐yes ☐no
        (one car for 3 persons)
    Are there natural barriers? ☐yes ☐no
        (rivers. etc.)
    Artificial barriers? ☐yes ☐no
        (expressways, etc.)

10. Visibility of site: On thoroughfare? ☐yes ☐no
     Corner site? ☐yes ☐no
     Neighborhood focus? Shopping center near? ☐yes ☐no
                              (desirable)
     School near? ☐yes ☐no
        (desirable)
     Slightly higher elevation? ☐yes ☐no Level? ☐yes ☐no
        (desirable)   (desirable)
     Site on nice, quiet side street? ☐yes ☐no (wrong location)
        (not desirable)
11. Soil: Soil test borings made? ☐yes ☐no
     Soil suitable for foundations? ☐yes ☐no
     Soil suitable for septic system? ☐yes ☐no

12. Price _____

Notes:

XIII

EVANGELISM FOR THE NEW CHURCH

 Evangelism for a new congregation is often more difficult than for an older, established congregation with adequate facilities. The new church must make every effort to reach out in its community. Otherwise the spiritual opportunities it offers to outsiders may be ignored. The minister must be an expounder of the Word, but he must also be a "door-knocker" if he is to challenge and to lead the infant congregation into an expanding program of evangelism.

It is my conviction there are at least six essential steps in an evangelistic program for a new church or any church for that matter. They are:

1. **Finding the lost and unchurched!** How? By following the example set by Christ! "For the Son of Man has come to seek and to save that which was lost" (Luke 19:10). Here are some excellent ways of finding the lost and unchurched:
   a. The Christian's friends and relatives (best).
   b. Bible School enrollment records.
   c. Letters from sister congregations.
   d. Silent roll call registration cards (Sunday to Sunday).
   e. Newcomers to the community (from welcome wagon, newspapers, Chamber of Commerce, observation of moving vans in your community and change of residents by the neighbors and Utilities' lists).
   f. Advertising . . . newspapers (daily), free community circulars, radio, TV, and college papers, and religious journals.
   g. A religious census—ask all questions first, leaving their name until the last.
   h. A telephone survey.
   i. Door-to-door visitation.
   j. Institutional visitation . . . hospitals, nursing homes, child-care centers, homes for the retired, etc.

k. Backyard Vacation Bible School.

l. Saturday afternoon "fun club" and Bible Story Hour.

m. Families in need.

n. "Have a Happy Day" card.

o. Newlyweds, new parents, deaths, job promotions, etc.

2. **Cultivating those found.** I Corinthians 3:6-10

a. The Friendly call.

We will all recognize the extreme lack of wisdom in rushing up to a total stranger, grabbing him by the lapels and blurting out, "Friend, are you saved?"

Perhaps the first contact will do no more than establish a friendly-acquaintance relationship. You will come to know the prospect. You will be able to analyze his personality, interests, and problems and thus be able to plan the next approach.

Be sure to keep a record of your visit.

b. The church-related call.

Know the information that previously was obtained, but leave the card or notebook in the car.

After a brief visit in which you establish a friendly climate, tell them that you want to invite them to the meetings of the church. Give an enthusiastic description of the church and its program.

It is well to have a presentation folder or some other piece of literature to help acquaint them with the church, its activities and message. Some find it valuable to have a small picture album to help them describe the church and its members.

3. **Teaching the prospect.** Matthew 28:18-20.

a. Make an appointment.

b. Take your Bible (marked) and a Bible for the prospect (or have the prospect use his own Bible, this is best).

c. Sit at a table and have your Bibles open in front of you.

d. Witness to what Christ means to you and how he has forgiven your sins.

e. Teach what the Bible says about sin, faith, repentance, confession, baptism, and living a Christian life.

f. Allow the prospect to ask questions and discuss what has been said.

g. After due teaching and discussion, seek to obtain a decision for Christ.

h. Lead the prospect toward the "Good Confession" and the need of being baptized for the remission of his sins.

i. The above is true if only the Bible is being used, if you are using other evangelistic teaching aids in addition to the Bible, such as filmstrips, tracts, charts, etc., you should adjust your teaching program accordingly.

j. Some Scriptures to use in personal evangelism (mark your Bible).

(1) All have sinned and fallen short of the glory of God. Romans 3:10, 23.

(2) The wages of sin. Romans 6:23 and Revelation 21:8.

(3) Man must hear the gospel to know what to do to be saved. Romans 10:17.

(4) Man must believe what he has heard. Acts 16:31, John 3:16, Hebrews 11:1-6.

(5) The prospect must repent. Acts 2:38, Luke 13:8.

(6) Then a confession of faith in Christ. Romans 10:9, Matthew 10:32-33, 16:16.

(7) There must be obedience in baptism (immersion into Christ)¡ Acts 2:38; 8:36-37; 22:16; I Peter 3:21; Galatians; Romans 6:3-4.

(8) We must be in Christ. John 3:16; 14:6; Acts 4:12; Romans 5:8; Revelation 3:20.

4. **Baptizing the taught.** Mark 16:16.

a. Jesus was baptized, Matthew 3:13-17, and He baptized, John 4:1-2.

b. Baptized in much water, John 3:22-23.

c. Must be born again, John 3:1-7.

d. The apostles baptized their converts, Acts 2:38,41; 10:44-48; 16:14-15, 30-33; 19:1-7, for the remission of sins and the gift of the Holy Spirit.

e. Paul was baptized, Acts 9:1-20 and taught the necessity of baptism, Romans 6:3-5; Galatians 3:27.

f. Peter taught that baptism is necessary to salvation, I Peter 3:20-21.

5. **Fellowship with those being taught.** (observable love) Fellowshipping with each other as Christ won persons. Some prerequisites for Christian fellowship:

a. Consecration.

b. Conviction, belief in a practical Christianity.

c. Confidence, let us develop a "holy confidence."

d. Radiance (enthusiasm), I love God! I love His people! I love you!

e. Friendliness, God's people are friendly, especially to the friendless.

f. Compassion, getting involved . . . putting love to work.

g. Empathy, putting ourselves in someone else's place.

h. Humility, "There but for the grace of God go I."

i. Self-control (meekness). Don't argue, you may win but you'll lose a soul.

j. Kindness, "Do unto others as you would have them do unto you."

6. **Teaching the convert,** Matthew 28:18-20, II Peter 1:1-11, II Timothy 3:15-17. How?

a. Bible School, Bible study and prayer meetings, and Bible Study groups.

b. Special classes at the church building and in the homes.

c. Special programs: missionary rallies, educational clinics, leadership clinics, and evangelistic meetings.

d. Bible-centered literature: books, tracts, magazines, etc.

e. Expository sermons.

f. Home devotions.

g. Daily Vacation Bible School.

h. Christian Service Camps for youth and adults.

i. In Christian colleges.

j. North American Christian Convention and other national conventions and rallies.

k. Camp retreats for men and women.

l. By example of Christian living.

m. By the examples of the elders, deacons, teachers, and the minister.

Sometimes it is difficult to pinpoint "Evangelism." It is my conviction that many facets of Christianity lend themselves to evangelism. The greeters and ushers can do much for the "on going" or the growth of the new church. Their concern, politeness and attention to details can do much to influence visitors to return or perhaps to accept Christ.

In the program of evangelism, as calling is done whether they are non-Christians, Christians who should transfer their membership or those who have become "spiritual dropouts," it is well to keep good records. Lertis R. Ellett, Basic Church Record Supplies, 5404 S. Prairie Ave., Lawndale, Calif., 90260 is a good source. Also enclosed in this book is a means of keeping records that I have borrowed from my good friend, Winston Zastrow of Clinton, Illinois. Please see pages 83-84.

Each time a call, a visit, is made upon a prospect a brochure describing the new church, stating its program and giving its location should be left at the home or with the individual. See pages 60-65 for examples of this brochure. This brochure should also be left in the door when no one is home. The interior of the brochure can be mimeographed with the church's special message. One of the special and effective ways of evangelism by a new congregation or any church is the "house-to-house" canvass or religious survey. This canvass can be conducted by the members, interested college students, Bible School classes and interested sister church members. A slower method is for the minister-evangelist to take his own "door-to-door" canvass, introducing himself and explaining that this is the method whereby he is seeking those whom the church can assist.

There are some general principles for effective results when conducting a religious survey. The new church must prepare or purchase adequate materials to be used. They will need survey cards, see pages 80-82, brochures that will identify the church and give its location, see pages 60-65. They will need for canvassing, street maps of the area to be canvassed, one for each team. The maps should be marked in such a way as to avoid any overlapping of efforts. Permission to canvass must often be obtained from the City hall or the police station. Sometimes a letter requesting permission to canvass must be written to the town council or its equivalent. This letter should be written about one month before the date established for the survey. It should also contain a sample of the materials to be used in the canvass. Publicity in the local papers in relationship to the canvass would be very helpful. Each person canvassing should be wearing a tag bearing his name and the church he represents. Those making the canvass will be briefed on what to expect, how to greet the householder, how to fill out the survey card, and how to complete their project. Here is a list of rules that have been compiled for "house-to-house" canvassing. Before the canvasser is sent out he should study these rules and familiarize himself with them.

1. Pray at each house as you approach the door and pray as you depart.
2. Make only a door call. Do not go inside the house . . . except under very unusual circumstances (for teenagers particularly).
3. If at all possible secure the desired information from an adult. If a child answers the door ask for the parent.
4. Speak up. Make your objective clear. Ask questions courteously.
5. Print legibly with pen or pencil. Cover every point requested. Of course, a person may refuse to answer some questions or all questions.
6. Use one survey card per family unit. Be alert to the fact that there might be two or more families at one address. Always confirm the address.
7. If no one is home, get the name from the mail box, door marker, or from a neighbor and record it along with the address. If house is vacant, indicate so on the reverse side of the survey card.
8. Be alert to all the needs of the home . . . sickness, a death in the family, family problems, a need for church membership, etc. Please record your observations on the reverse side of the survey card.
9. Note on the reverse side of the survey card any personal opinions concerning the possibility of reaching the home or individual for Christ and His Church.
10. Thank the householder for his cooperation and be sure and leave a brochure or a tract.
11. REMEMBER YOU ARE DOING THE LORD'S WORK! Approach the door with confidence and with a smile. Your opportunity is important to the Lord, to your church and to you. You are not a solicitor or a salesman. You will be discovering precious souls who need the Lord and can be led to Christ. EXPECT COOPERATION AND YOU WILL GET IT!!!!!!!

SOME IMPORTANT "DO'S!"

1. Do Smile . . . and smile . . . and smile.
2. Do be positive.
3. Do remember why you are there.
4. Do leave something at every house.
5. Do remember names, faces, etc.
6. Do look him or her "in the eye."
7. Do ask proper questions.
8. Do ask for what you want.
9. Do make the person feel at ease.
10. Do mention the children, ages, etc.
11. Do take down all information.
12. Do be natural.
13. Do be flexible.

14. Do be thankful even when someone says "No" . . . for at least you secured a response.
15. Do witness to your faith.
16. Do witness concerning your church.
17. Do be willing to repeat questions and to explain patiently.
18. Do leave a tract or information folder even if no one was home.
19. Do watch your map and stay within its boundaries.
20. Do carry your Bible . . . in your hand or in your pocket.

SOME IMPORTANT DON'TS!
1. Don't forget to let God work through you.
2. Don't forget to pray and pray.
3. Don't judge or argue.
4. Don't chew gum or eat candy, etc.
5. Don't walk on the lawn.
6. Don't place anything in the mail box.
7. Don't spend too much time at each house.
8. Don't be negative or complain.
9. Don't talk over the person's head.
10. Don't talk about yourself.
11. Don't be afraid to say, "I don't know."
12. Don't forget we don't have all the answers.
13. Don't forget your materials.
14. Don't forget your pen or to sharpen your pencil.
15. Don't forget your Bible.
16. Don't cross over into other areas.
17. Don't forget the time and meet your driver or the bus at the appointed hour.

The "house-to-house" canvass has been completed. Now, what about the follow-up? Every prospect and suspect must be contacted by a trained and spiritually minded person. At least two sets of permanent file cards should be prepared. One set according to name (alphabetically) and the other according to the street or road. One new church also records all the cards according to the religion of the household, all households or individuals contacted. Follow-up calls on those canvassed should be made as soon as possible. If too much time elapses, the church will lose much of the advantage of the canvass.

For a card (form) that can be used in calling on those contacted and also keeping permanent records, please see pages 83-84. Both sides will be useable on this calling card or record.

For further study and expertise on the subject of Church growth, I recommend without reservation, the following books by Dr. Paul Benjamin. They are, *How in the World* and *The Growing Congregation*. In these books Dr. Benjamin has shown us principles which allow us to launch out in making the new church grow effecitvely and dynamically. His books are logical scriptural and practical. There is a study book or work book available for *The Growing Congregation*.

WITNESS-SURVEY

Street	Number	City or Suburb	Date

Hello, I'm _____ (and this is _____).
I'm (We're) from the _____ Church. I'm (We're)
making a religious survey of the families in our area because we
want to serve others better. Will you please help us by answering a
few brief questions?

1. Are there any children or young people living here?

Age   Grade   What are their names?

_____
_____
_____
_____
_____

2. What is their last name? _____

3. Do they regularly attend Sunday School?
YES _____   NO _____

If "no,"   Would you consider permitting them to at-
then ask: tend our school?
YES _____   NO _____

If "yes,"   Do they need transportation?
then ask:
YES _____   NO _____

4. Are you attending church anywhere now?
YES _____   NO _____
If "yes,"   Which one? _____
then ask: (Specific church & community)

How often do you attend:
once a week? _____   once a month? _____
once a year? _____
Are you a member? YES _____   NO _____

5. Is your husband/wife (cross out incorrect word) attending
church anywhere? YES _____   NO _____
If "yes,"   Which one? _____
then ask: (Specific church & community)
How often does (he/she) attend:
once a month? _____   once a year? _____
Is (he/she) a member? YES _____   NO _____

6. Are there other adults living here?

7. What is the family name at this address?

Information _____

8. Would you be interested in a home Bible study group?
YES _____   NO _____

9. Would you be interested in a Bible correspondence course?
YES _____   NO _____

10. May I (we) inquire what you believe about Jesus
Christ?
Note: here may be the best place to share your own
testimony.

Not at home _____   Information refused _____
Vacant house _____   Responsive _____
Not responsive _____   Other _____

Name of surveyor _____

LCC Press, Box 176, Lincoln, Illinois 62656

Note: The above "Witness-survey" form has been included through the
courtesy of Dr. Paul Benjamin. It has been taken from his book *How in
the World.* This form was tested many times in Chicago surveys and
has proven very effective.

House number _____ Street _____ City _____

Hello! I am from the _____ and this religious survey is being taken to increase our effectiveness in serving this community.

Would you say you attend religious services: Every week _____?

Every 2 weeks _____? Seldom _____? Never _____? Other _____?

Of what church are you a member or prefer? (circle)

Catholic   Lutheran   Baptist   Presbyterian   Episcopalian   Christian   Methodist

Church of Christ   Bible   Other _____

Number of children in home? (circle)   1   2   3   4   5   6   7

Teenagers in the home? (circle)   13   14   15   16   17   18   19 _____

College age in home? (circle)   1   2   3   4   5   6   _____ (Age)

Would you be interested in a Home Bible Study Course?   Yes   No

Family Name _____

_____

Use other side of card for special information

81

ADDRESS _____ floor_____

(street number) (city or suburb) apt. _____

DATE _____ Not Home ☐ Vacant ☐ Refused ☐ Other _____

First Name	Member	Attends	Prefers	List specific church & community
Mr. _____	☐	☐	☐	_____
Mrs. _____	☐	☐	☐	_____
Other _____	☐	☐	☐	_____
_____	☐	☐	☐	_____

No. of Children Names Name of Sunday School

Sunday School { Pre-School 1-5 _____ _____

Grades 6-14 _____ _____

High School 15-18 _____ _____

Where attending now _____

(church) (location)

Adults attend : Regularly _____ Occasionally _____ Seldom _____ Never _____

Children attend : Regularly _____ Occasionally _____ Seldom _____ Never _____

FAMILY NAME _____ phone _____

Use other side of card for special information

82

Name _____

Last _____ First _____

Address _____ Ph: _____

ADULT AGE RANGE (Estimated) 18-25 25-30 30-40 40-50 50-60 Over 60

CHILDREN'S NAMES   Age   Sex

_____ | _____

_____ | _____

_____ | _____

EMPLOYED _____ HAS ATTENDED HERE _____

INTERESTS _____

MEMBERS ACQUAINTED WITH _____

RELIGIOUS BACKGROUND _____

FIRST VISIT—VISITORS _____ DATE _____

SECOND VISIT—VISITORS _____ DATE _____

THIRD VISIT—VISITORS _____ DATE _____

"Go ye therefore, and teach all nations, baptizing them in the name of the Father, and of the Son, and of the Holy Ghost: Teaching them to observe all things whatsoever I have commanded you: and, lo, I am with you alway, even unto the end of the world." (Matthew 28:19,20) (KJV)

(OVER)

83

REPORTS ON CONTACTS MADE

Include any comments you feel would be helpful for the next visitor to know. Give suggestions on what should be done next. Comment on the extent to which the purpose of the call was accomplished. State any problems faced that you would like to discuss before making another visit.

FIRST VISIT (Date made:)

SECOND VISIT (Date made:)

THIRD VISIT (Date made:)

FOURTH VISIT (Date made:)

XIV

THE NEW CHURCH FUNCTIONING EFFECTIVELY

 The Apostle Paul speaks of the functioning church (mature church) in Ephesians 4:11-16 and in I Corinthians, chapters 12, 13, 14. The new church is beginning to function properly (maturing) when it becomes self-supporting, when it is contributing at least ten per cent of its funds to missions, and when its leaders and members are "building up the body of Christ" with the "proper working of each individual part, causing the growth of the body for the building up of itself in love."

Without a doubt the functioning church will now be ready for the selection (election) of elders and deacons. Perhaps two years have elapsed since the church began and a leadership committee has been functioning. This has been good training and a proving ground for men who may "desire" the office of elder or deacon. Let the congregation select a committee to review the qualifications of men who may desire to be elders or deacons. This committee should also receive the suggestions of the congregation as to men they deem qualified. Available on page 87 is a method of gaining suggestions from the congregation. Procedures for selection of men for the office will be in the By-Laws or must be evolved by the Leadership committee or the congregation.

Each congregation should also elect at least three trustees, especially if property is involved. This will be a state required office.

Other officers of the church such as treasurer, financial secretary, church clerk, Bible School superintendent, congregational chairman, etc. will also be elected according to the procedures decided upon or set forth in the by-laws.

All business meetings are to be conducted in accordance to the by-laws or according to agreed upon procedures. See page 88 as to a suggested agenda for conducting business meetings of the congregation.

The mature congregation will carry adequate insurance on its minister (retirement, disability, hospital, etc.), its buildings, and protection for the congregation in case of mishaps around and in the buildings.

Christian education as well as evangelism will be a major endeavor of the functional church. The church will be programmed to be taught and to teach. A church program such as this never "just happens." Where it exists, it means there is dedicated, knowledgeable leadership, the preacher included, devoting themselves to **causing** the church program to succeed. A successful workable church program of Christian education means:

1. The congregation has realized the importance of remaking inner lives of individuals by the power of the Holy Spirit and the living Christ.
2. The leadership of the church is composed of spiritual men and women who are of "good repute, full of the Spirit and of wisdom." (Acts 6:3, Weymouth's New Testament in Modern Speech)
3. This congregation is planning to use all of its facilities and manpower to organize and execute God's plans and programs as revealed in His Word.
4. The church will be committed to careful and visionary planning with a capable and dedicated membership seeking to expand God's Kingdom here on earth.

The church that does not plan a total Christian educational program (more than Sunday School) for its membership, is planning for mediocrity and perhaps failure.

Christian education for the mature congregation must include Biblical indoctrination, stewardship, Christian leadership courses, teacher training, expository teaching and preaching, home Bible studies, sessions on prayer, etc. It must be geared to reach all ages of the congregation, from the cradle roll to the "golden agers."

The preacher (evangelist, minister) is the key man in the church, particularly the new church. It goes without saying that he must be a man of God. He must be motivated by God's Spirit! He must be a "self-starter" as he observes the world on a collision course with the church and all things spiritual. He must realize the truth of John's statement "Do not love the world, nor the things in the world. If anyone loves the world, the love of the Father is not in him. For all that is in the world, the lust of the flesh and the lust of the eyes and the boastful pride of life, is not from the Father, but is from the world" (I John 2:15-16).

In the selection of a preacher the utmost care must be exercised. A pulpit committee should be appointed. Procedures in calling a preacher should be devised, if by-laws are not in force. See pages 89-92 as to some guidelines in calling a minister. (From Pearl Willis' "Elders' and Deacons' Manual.") If a contract is signed (many preachers are called on verbal agreements) a sample is included, see pages 93-94.

Inasmuch as your congregation has reached physical and spiritual maturity, may I issue a challenge to you? Why not lead in planting a new congregation in an area near you that is unreached? One that is founded and dedicated to the principles of restoring the church according to the teachings found in the New Testament? To me this is the ultimate sign of true maturity in Christ.

NOMINATION GUIDE FOR
SELECTION OF ELDERS AND DEACONS

Having given prayerful consideration to the teaching of the Scriptures, as contained in I Timothy 3:1-13 and Titus 1:6-9, and recognizing that the Holy Spirit said elders and deacons "must be" the kind of men He describes, I nominate the following men:

For Elders:

	1.	2.	3.	4.	5.
Above reproach					
A fine work he desires to do					
Husband of one wife					
Temperate					
Prudent					
Respectable					
Hospitable					
Able to teach					
Not addicted to wine					
Not pugnacious					
Gentle					
Free from the love of money					
Uncontentious					
Manages his own household well					
Not a new convert					
Good reputation outside the church					
Loving what is good					
Devout					
Holding fast the faithful word					
Self-controlled					
Not quick-tempered					
Just					
Sensible					

Deacons:

	1.	2.	3.	4.	5.	6.	7.	8.
Men of dignity								
Not double-tongued								
Not addicted to much wine								
Not fond of sordid gain								
Holding to the mystery of faith with a clear conscience								
Let them be tested								
Beyond reproach								
Husbands of one wife								
Good managers of children and their own households								

AGENDA FOR CONDUCTING BUSINESS

1. Devotions and prayer. (begin on announced time)

2. Welcome and introductions.

3. Secretary's report.

4. Treasurer's report.

5. Minister's report.

6. Committee reports:

7. Old business:

8. New business:

9. Announcements, etc.

10. Motion to adjourn.

11. Benediction.

12. Fellowship and refreshments.

GUIDELINES FOR SELECTING A MINISTER

The following information is for your confidential use in interviewing a prospective candidate for the pulpit of the local congregation in which you are serving. It will be only as useful as you make it by careful observation and complete honesty in expressing your opinions, and by the accuracy used in accumulating the facts and information from all sources. May God bless you in this sacred trust of securing a capable servant of the Lord for His people (Pearl Willis).

Prospect's name _____

Your Personal observation:

1. Does he make a good appearance? _____

2. Does he meet people well? _____

3. Is he friendly? _____

4. Does he have any annoying habit? _____

5. Does he preside well in the pulpit? _____

6. Does he seem well organized? _____ In conducting services? ____

   In sermon content? _____

7. Does he use Scripture in sermons? _____

   In an effective way? _____

   As his authority? _____

8. Is he evangelistic? _____

9. How do you feel he would be as a teacher for mid-week services

   or for a Bible School class? _____

10. Does he seem interested in the church members? _____

    Speak to children? _____

    Call members by name? _____

11. Does his speaking seem to be mature? _____

    Get singsongy? _____

12. Does he appear to be mature? _____

    Is his speaking pleasing? _____

    Appear to be monotonous? _____

89

13. Does he use illustrations well?_____

14. Is his message easily understood?_____

15. Do you feel that the members of the church listened well? _____

16. Do you feel your congregation would respond well to his

    preaching _____

17. Do you have any reservations about recommending this minister to your

    people? _____

18. Does he seem to be punctual? _____

19. What age do you think him to be?_____

20. Made additional comments: _____

    _____

Family:

1. Wife's name?_____

2. Wife's age? _____

3. Has she attended College?_____ Where? _____

4. Is she friendly? _____

5. Does she assist her husband in his ministry in a special way?

   _____

6. How many children? _____

Education and Background information:

1. Public school attended?_____

2. Bible college attended? _____

3. Other schools attended? _____

4. Is he continuing to develop his knowledge? _____

   If so, in what ways?_____

   _____

5. How long has he been engaged in his present ministry? _____

6. How has the average attendance fared during his ministry? _____

   When he came? _____ Now?_____

7. How many additions has the church recorded during his ministry?

   Baptisms? _____ Transfers? _____

8. How has the congregational income fared during his ministry? ____

   When he came? _____ Now? _____

   Missions _____

9. How many calls does he make during a month? _____

10. Have you asked for an organizational chart of the church or discussed the organizational work with him? If so, how do you feel he would be as an administrator? _____

    _____

11. Does he have an assistant or does he desire one? _____

12. Why does he seem interested in leaving this location? _____

    _____

13. Does the reason seem logical? _____

14. Where else has he ministered? _____

15. Why did he terminate these earlier ministries? _____

16. Are you satisfied with his record of stability? _____

17. What is his present income? _____

18. What will be his needs?_____

    _____

Health:

1. Does he appear to be in good health? _____

2. Did he mention any illness? _____

3. Has he missed much work during the past year because of illness?

   _____

4. Does he have any hobbies to help relieve tension and give him a change of pace?

_____

_____

Faith: (Questions to be asked one desiring to be your minister.)

1. Would you define your faith in Christ? Do you believe that He is God's only begotten Son? Do you firmly believe, without reservation, in the virgin birth? Do you believe in His bodily resurrection from the grave?

2. Please define your belief concerning the Scriptures. Do you believe that they are inspired of God? Do you believe that they are accurate in presenting God's will for man? Do you believe that they are sufficient as our rule of faith and practice?

3. What are your convictions concerning the necessity for immersion and the observance of the Lord's Supper?

4. Would you explain to us your belief in the Holy Spirit? Do you believe in speaking in tongues today? Do you feel that we today receive the baptism of the Holy Spirit? Do you believe that miracles are being performed today by men under the power of the Holy Spirit?

Co-Operative Works:

1. What is your attitude toward interdenominational work? Ministerial Associations? Good Friday services? Other union services?

2. Would you care to mention any of our brotherhood agencies, missionary or otherwise, with which you or the church you serve could not co-operate?

3. How do you feel about national, regional, county-wide co-operation among Christian Churches, Christian Service Camps, and Evangelistic Associations, etc.?

4. How many revivals, speaking engagements, etc. would you desire to participate in during a year?

PROPOSED CONTRACT BETWEEN _____ ,

MINISTER AND THE _____

This contract will be presented to the congregation for final approval. This is not a legal document but merely an agreement of terms to be for information and reference between the minister and the congregation.

1. SALARY: An amount of $_____ per week shall be paid.

2. UTILITIES: All utilities used by the minister and his family shall be paid by the church.

3. MILEAGE: The minister shall be given the amount of $_____ per month or week as travel expense for travel done in behalf of the congregation.

4. PHONE: The basic rate of one private line and an amount to cover all church-related toll calls shall be paid. The minister will pay for his private toll calls.

5. CONVENTION ALLOWANCE: The sum of $_____ per year shall be available for the minister to be reimbursed for convention expenses of a church-related convention. The expenses reimbursed will include mileage, housing, food and related expenses. This money will not be available unless the minister attends a convention.

6. INSURANCE: An amount of $_____ per week will be set aside by the church treasurer for:

7. VACATION: The minister shall be given two weeks* each year, beginning in _____.

8. REVIVALS: The minister shall be allowed time to participate in two revivals or evangelistic meetings each year, 2 "one" week meetings.

9. CAMP: The minister shall be allowed two weeks per year including two Sunday evenings* to be involved in church camp.

10. DAY OFF: One day per week shall be designated as the minister's "day off." The day will be determined by the minister and announced to the congregation.

11. CONTRACT REVIEW: The salary and benefits outlined above shall be reviewed in December of each year. At this time, a re-evaluation of the entire church program shall also be made and additional goals established as needed.

12. MOVING EXPENSES: All reasonable moving expenses shall be paid by the congregation.

13. TERMINATION: A notice of sixty days shall be given by either party in order to terminate employment unless other arrangements are made by mutual consent of both parties involved.

Approved by the _____ on _____ 19___.
            (church)

Signed: _____

Signed: _____
                                Minister

*Indicates Sundays during which the minister will be absent and the church will provide a pulpit supply.

94

XV.
PARENTING (mothering) NEW CHURCHES

There is no one single way to begin a new congregation. Each situation demands careful thought and evaluation. It is my valued opinion that every church should at sometime in its history reproduce itself. Many, many churches could do this over and over again. A very noted minister, educator and church planter, now dead, C. J. Sharp, refers to this as the church "swarming." A very apt reference because the established congregation sends forth a rather large nucleus to another area.

The Church who will "parent" another church will experience tremendous blessings and will soon grow beyond what they were before the "blessed event." Here are some of the blessings or rich rewards that will accrue to the parenting church.

1. By becoming deeply involved in the beginning of our Lord's Church in a new community or municipality, you will be bringing the opportunity for others to know and to accept Christ as their Saviour.
2. You will be developing additional leadership ability and skills in both congregations.
3. You will become totally immersed in the activities of the Body of Christ the Church...making it possible for you and others to participate in many new and different programs and activities of the new church and/or the mothering church.
4. You will have the satisfaction of knowing that you have made it possible to plant a new church. These memories will remain to excite you for the rest of your life.
5. As precious souls are won, ministerial and missionary recruits are enlisted, teachers are found and developed and you will receive a deep and everlasting blessing from assisting in their discovery and will share in their victories.
6. For most families, individuals or churches, this will be the first time they have had the privilege of participating in the establishment of a new church. Most Christians have never pioneered in the planting of a "spiritual beachhead" for the redemption of mankind and to the glory of Chirst. It can be and certainly will be the most exciting and greatest adventure of their lives. With the possible exception of marriage or the

birth of a child into a family, but, of course, parenting a new church is much like either one or both.

Perhaps the ideal way to parent a new church is to find an area or community nearby or at a distance without a Christian Church (target area). Then a program of concern for the target area could be launched in the congregation. Over a period of months reasons for parenting a new church in the target area could be given from the pulpit, by the elders and deacons, the Bible School teachers, from the newsletter, etc. Here are some very excellent reasons for a congregation to become involved in parenting a new church.

1. A new church will provide a "Family of God" for the Christians who have moved into another area, city or community. Those who move away, some say that one in five families move each year, will not be lost to Christ and His Church.
2. A new church brings the beautiful message of Christ and His love for mankind to new cities and communities that are being established throughout our nation.
3. Cultural and ethnic groups and peoples have, often times, serious problems in identifying with our established churches. Parenting a new church in an ethnic neighborhood can be a very satisfactory method of evangelizing that community. The Central Christian Church, Harvey, IL, Robert Sloniger, minister, had a number of Hispanics meeting with them, they assisted them in planting a new church in Blue Island, IL, where a large number of Hispanics lived.
4. Most people, unless they are dedicated Christians, will not "commute" to church services. They will commute to work six days-a-week but are not willing to drive out of their area to church services. Parenting a church in the target area brings the church, the gospel, to their doors.
5. It is almost impossible to reach your neighbors for Christ by transporting them to "church" in another city, again, the new church brings Christ to them.

In preparation for the blessed event of planned parenthood for a new church, the leadership and the congregation must evaluate and examine anew their concept of evangelism. Perhaps the following questions will assist in this recommended procedure.

1. What is evangelism? Suggested reading and study would be Luke 10:1-24; John 4; the 28 chapters of the Book of Acts of the Apostles.
2. How is evangelism best accomplished? Study in depth Acts 8.
3. What concept do you as a leader in Christ's Church have of the Church? Read and study I Corinthians 12:12-31; Ephesians 4:1-16, 5:23-33; Colossians 1:9-29.
4. Do you accept the Church as God's instrument to save the world through Christ? (a) A close study of the Book of Acts reveals the beginning of the Church of Jesus Christ and the continuous spread of Christianity. (b) Christians reproducing Christians, Acts 8:4 "Those who had been scattered, preached the Word wherever they went," (c) Churches reproducing churches, Acts 13:1-20:38, Paul and Barnabas

were sent forth from Antioch to establish churches in city after city.

5. Is evangelism the heartbeat of the Church, your church? If so: (a) This keeps the church alive and well. The Church is always just one generation away from extinction. (b) Every community, city or area can be and must be evangelized by planting a Church based on the New Testament in it.

6. Is the "local church the "end" or is it the "means" of evangelizing the world? It is my conviction, based upon a study of the Bible, the Word of God, and particularly the New Testament, the "local" church is the "means" whereby we as Christians serve together in the "Body of Christ," the Church, to win the world for Christ! So therefore, today, not tomorrow, we must by faith launch out into new cities, new communities, subdivisions, cultures and areas to plant the Church of our Lord.

With the foregoing in mind, here are some practical procedures to be used in the great adventure of parenting a new church, to be used by the elders/board, etc.

1. Examine the motives for planting a new church. To win souls and to have Christian fellowship are the proper motives. The improper motives are "fight" and/or "flight."

2. Make constant use of the "Step-by-Step procedures in New Church planting" as outlined in this book, (Growing New Churches by Carl W. Moorhous).

3. Appoint a special prayer committee for this extra special venture in faith. Above everything else, the parenting church should pray constantly and fervently for her offspring. The new church must also be involved in prayer sessions. Let the entire project be bathed in prayer. Seek the prayers of sister congregations.

4. Share the ambitions, hopes and dreams of the leadership with the total congregation and seek their input and blessings.

5. Publicize the opportunity for enlistment or participation in the new church, which will be open to all.

6. Decide, if possible, and publicize the target area where the new church will be serving or at least where they will be worshiping and hold Bible School.

7. Start weekly Bible Study, using the Book of Acts, and prayer time, in a home in the target area. This could be held in the building of the mothering congregation if necessary. These sessions can be led by the minister(s) or the elders.

8. Following the Bible Studies should be planning sessions for the structure of the new church (see page 17 of this book).

9. Select a special committee from the parenting church to meet with the nucleus of the new church and they will be a liaison between the two. The special committee would not have any authority or power to vote in business sessions of the new church.

10. Allow the new church to select a beginning date and then publicize the date throughout the parenting congregation as much as possible

and in every way possible. Tell the good news in the church's newsletter at every publication, from the pulpit, on the radio, through the TV, use the national brotherhood religious publications and the regional newspapers.

11. Invite sister congregations to share in your joys and opportunities to parent a new church. They can assist you in many ways.

12. If there is an Evangelistic Association or Felllowship in the area or state, invite them to participate in some important capacity. Their experience in new church planting will be very helpful.

13. Dramatize the beginning of the new church by offering a special invitation in the worship services of mother church the Sunday prior to the Sunday the church is to open its charter. Develop a tremendous program around the leadership of the parent church and the nucleus of the offspring.

14. Maintaining fellowship and communication between the "parent" and the "offspring" is very important. This can be done by pulpit exchange, teacher exchange, leadership exchange, joint services, special services, etc. They can encourage one another and share victories and achievements.

15. Parenting a new church can lead to great stewardship opportunities for the parent church. She can assist in calling the full-time minister/evangelist, in purchasing a building site and in erection of a house of worship. Planting a new church gives both congregations a greater opportunity to share their many blessings with the Lord and His people. This will be time, talent and money.

16. Through all the activities of planting a new church, by the infant and the mother, we dare not lose sight of Christ as the Head of the Church and the Saviour of the Body, Ephesians 1:20-23, 2:18-22, 5:23-33; Colossians 1:9-29.

In parenting a new congregation there are some very worthwhile axioms to follow:

1. A strong nucleus builds a strong church. Leadership is so important!

2. Grab great opportunities when and while you can.

3. Don't be concerned about losing some of your outstanding leaders. God will raise up new ones! Just build the Kingdom of God here on earth.

4. Established churches with established credit have an opportunity and an obligation to use that credit to plant other Christian Churches according to the New Testament pattern. New churches have no "track record" with banks, etc., thus find it almost impossible to borrow money.

5. There is never a "good" or "perfect" time to parent a new church. **Now** is the accepted time.

6. MISSIONS must be a part of the new church's program from the very beginning.

7. The "parenting" church must be willing to lend oversight and the new church must be willing to accept it.

8. A stagnant or non-growth target area will make for a slow growth by

the new church.

9. An experienced, capable minister/evangelist is the best investment a new church can make, especially when beginning.

10. Establishing a new church could actually save the parent congregation much money and increase its spiritual and numerical growth.

11. In parenting a new church it will be wise for the parent to seek advice and assistance from nearby sister congregations.

12. The parent congregation will need to provide committed people in such areas as: music, worship, publicity, supply preaching, teaching, calling, etc. Some will only be temporary, perhaps.

13. Start living by faith in both the churches, new and established...become spiritual pioneers:

"Doubt sees the obstacles, Faith sees the way.
Doubt sees the darkest night, Faith sees the day.
Doubt dreads to take a step, Faith soars on high.
Doubt questions, 'Who believes?' Faith answers, 'I.'"

14. Here are some questions, however, that need to be answered in parenting new churches. **Who supplies the seed?** God does, through His Word! **Who sows the seed?** God does through His people! **What is the field?** The world and its people! **What is the result?** NEW LIFE IN CHRIST...THE CHURCH, HIS CHURCH! (borrowed and adapted from Wally Blanchard.)

We must plant and parent new churches! We can not win America, not to mention the world, by renewing and expanding our existing churches, as much as this is needed. There are many, many reasons for planting new churches but here are four:

1. Christ commanded it in the Great Commission, Matthew 28:18-20; Acts 1:8.

2. The Apostles and the New Testament church leaders did it, see Acts of the Apostles. They were led by the Holy Spirit in doing so, Acts 13:1-4, etc.

3. Evangelism is only effective where those who are won to Christ become absorbed into a vital Christian fellowship...the Church. Man can not live alone, nor can a "born-again" man live to himself.

4. Penetration of another city, community or culture for Christ is not achieved by transporting people to an established congregation in another city or area. Penetration can only be achieved by establishing a new church in the unreached cities and communities.

Acknowledgement of suggestions and ideas must be given some men, evangelists and good friends of mine who have led in "parenting" (mothering) new churches. They are Robert Sloniger, Dave Buche, Earl Ferguson, Dave Taylor, Richard Sargent, Fred Smith, Jr., Karl Roberts, Frank Forehand, Andrew Pryer, and Wally Blanchard.

NOTE: There is a film available on parenting new churches. It is valuable in challenging a congregation to launch in faith to establish a new church. It is entitled "Planned Parenthood for Churches." You can rent it from Church Growth, 150 South Los Robles, Suite 600, Pasadena, CA 91101, Phones: 800/423-4844 (in California 213/449-4400).

PRELIMINARY GUIDELINES FOR "MOTHERING" A NEW CHURCH

1. DETERMINE IF THE NEED EXISTS.

Discussion by leaders of the "Mothering" congregation.

Analyze the membership of the "Mothering" church.

Evaluate the effectiveness of the "Mother" church in a given area.

Needs and growth potential of the target area for a new church.

2. PRAYER BY LEADERSHIP AND THE CONGREGATION

Designated day and constantly for God's guidance.

"Zero in" on the target area and persons and families.

3. NEW CHURCH PROMOTION.

By minister/preacher/evangelist.

By elders and deacons.

By teachers.

By members.

Organizing evangelist.

Religious journals.

From pulpit.

Newsletters.

Bulletins.

Displays.

Classes.

4. MEETINGS FOR DISCUSSION.

Set a date.

Led by organizing evangelist.

Attended by all or designated leadership.

For all members with some interest.

Advertise within sister congregations.

Devotions and prayer.

5. MEETINGS PLANNING THE NEW CHURCH

Once a week. Led by organizing evangelist. Devotions/prayer.

Explanations and review.

Use and study the book on "Growing New Churches."

Sign up for membership in new church.

Temporary committees.

Temporary officers.

Meeting place selected.

First day for formal services.

Charter is signed.

6. CONTINUING THE GROWTH OF THE NEW CHURCH.

House-to-house canvass of target area.

Teaching/preaching/baptizing/fellowship.

Visitation.

SUGGESTED BOOKS AND MATERIALS FOR
IDEAS IN CHURCH PLANTING

Acts, The; or Acts of the Apostles. Any New Testament.

Alexander, John W., *Managing Our Work,* Downers Grove, Illinois 60515: Inter-Varsity Press, 1972.

Benjamin, Paul, *The Growing Congregation,* Lincoln, Illinois: Lincoln Christian College Press, 1972.

Benjamin, Paul, *How in the World?,*Lincoln, Illinois 62656: Lincoln Christian College Press, 1973.

Brown, Arvil, *Building Sites and Buildings,* 1130 Chris J Dr., Lansing, Michigan 48197: Unpublished.

Ellis, Joe, *The Personal Evangelist,* Cincinnati, Ohio 45231: Standard Publishing.

Felton, Virgil, *A Manual for New Church Evangelism.* Grand Ledge, Michigan 48917: New Churches of Christ Evangelism, 1974.

Hargrove, Earl C., *The Road to Satisfaction,* Lincoln, Illinois 62656: Lincoln Christian College Press, 1969.

Hodges, Melvin L., *Grow Toward Leadership,* Chicago, Illinois: Moody Press 1969.

Hodges, Melvin L., *A Guide to Church Planting,* Chicago, Illinois: Moody Press, 1973.

Jacobs, Vernon, *What We Believe,* Cincinnati, Ohio 45231: Standard Publishing, 1963.

Longenecker, Harold L., *Building Town and Country Churches,* Chicago, Illinois: Moody Press, 1973.

Leach, William H., *Handbook of Church Management,* Englewood Cliffs, New Jersey: Prentice-Hall, Inc., 1963.

Leavitt, Guy P., *Superintend with Success,* Cincinnati, Ohio 45321: Standard Publishing.

Little, Paul E., *How to Give Away Your Faith,* Downers Grove, Illinois 60515: Inter-Varsity Press, 1966.

Mains, David R., *Full Circle,* Waco, Texas: Word Books, 1972.

McGavran, Donald A. and Win Arn, *How to Grow a Church,* Glendale, California: B/L Publications, Regal Books, 1973.

Schaeffer, Francis A., *The Mark of the Christian,* Downers Grove, Illinois 60515: Inter-Varsity Press, 1970.

Shepard, C. E., *New Church Evangelism* (A Study Book), Kempton, Indiana: Mission Services Press, 1969.

Shannon, Robert C., *The New Testament Church,* Cincinnati, Ohio 45321: Standard Publishing, 1964.

Stedman, Ray C., *Body Life,* Glendale, California 91029: Regal Books Division, G/L Publications.

Wade, John W., *Pioneers of the Restoration Movement,* Cincinnati, Ohio 45321: Standard Publishing.

Willis, P. A., *Elders' and Deacons' Manual,* 8634 Cottonwood Dr., Cincinnati, Ohio 45218: Christian Leadership Services, 1968.

"Your Church" (magazine), The Religious Publishing Co., 198 Allendale Road, King of Prussia, Pa., 19406.

"Visualized Bible Study Series" (Visual Aids for evangelism), Gospel Services, Inc., P. O. Box 12302, Houston, Texas 77017.

Church Growth Services, 120 Callander St., South Bend, Indiana 46614.

"Christian Standard" (magazine) Standard Publishing, Cincinnati, Ohio 45321.

National Church Growth Research Center, Dr. Paul Benjamin, director, Box 3760, Washington, D. C. 20007.